WATCH *and Be* READY

OTHER TITLES BY BRENT L. TOP

Books

Doctrinal Commentary on the Book of Mormon, vols. 1–4
(with Robert L. Millet and Joseph Fielding McConkie)

*Follow the Living Prophets: Timely Reasons for
Observing Prophetic Counsel in the Last Days*
(with Larry E. Dahl and Walter Bowen)

Forgiveness: Christ's Priceless Gift

LDS Beliefs: A Doctrinal Reference
(with Robert L. Millet, Andrew C. Skinner, and Camille Fronk Olson)

A Peculiar Treasure: Old Testament Messages for Our Day

*The Shield of Faith: The Power of Religion in the
Lives of LDS Youth and Young Adults*
(with Bruce Chadwick and Richard J. McClendon)

What's on the Other Side?

When You Can't Do It Alone

Talks on CD

Quenching Spiritual Thirst

Strengthened by His Hand

*What's on the Other Side:
What the Gospel Teaches Us about the Spirit World*

WATCH *and* *Be* READY

Preparing Spiritually for the Second Coming of Christ

BRENT L. TOP

DESERET
BOOK

SALT LAKE CITY, UTAH

WATCH *and* *Be* READY

Preparing Spiritually for the Second Coming of Christ

BRENT L. TOP

DESERET
BOOK

SALT LAKE CITY, UTAH

Images on pages x and xi are artifacts from the private collection of Brent and Wendy Top, photographed by Richard Crookston. Image on page 1 © rolfo/Getty Images; page 15 © georgeclerk/Getty Images; page 33 © Syldavia/Getty Images; page 109 © bgfotos/Getty Images. All images used by permission.

Library of Congress Cataloging-in-Publication Data

Names: Top, Brent L., author.
Title: Watch and be ready : preparing spiritually for the second coming of Christ / Brent L. Top.
Description: Salt Lake City, Utah : Deseret Book, [2018] | Includes bibliographical references and index.
Identifiers: LCCN 2018006935 | ISBN 9781629724508 (hardbound : alk. paper)
Subjects: LCSH: Second Advent. | Mormon Church—Doctrines. | The Church of Jesus Christ of Latter-day Saints—Doctrines.
Classification: LCC BX8643.S43 T67 2018 | DDC 236/.9—dc23
LC record available at https://lccn.loc.gov/2018006935

Printed in the United States of America
Edwards Brothers Malloy, Ann Arbor, MI

10 9 8 7 6 5 4 3 2 1

CONTENTS

CONTENTS

ACKNOWLEDGMENTS

Several people have played important roles in the process of publishing this book. It was not a book that I had intended to write, but I am grateful that Jana Erickson at Deseret Book strongly encouraged me to do so. She wouldn't let me off the hook. Her suggestions and feedback were valuable throughout the process. Without her prodding, this book would not have been written. Likewise, Lisa Roper, product director at Deseret Book, was extraordinarily helpful. I appreciate greatly her valuable counsel and continual support and encouragement. I am also grateful for the careful work of my editor, Emily Watts. I appreciate the professionalism of all on the Deseret Book team. In addition, I wish to thank several of my colleagues in Religious Education at Brigham Young University (you know who you are) who reviewed various drafts of the manuscript and helped improve this work. Most of all, I express my appreciation for my wife, Wendy, not only for her important contributions to this book but for her continual love and support of me.

PREFACE

When our family lived in the Holy Land while I was teaching at the BYU Jerusalem Center for Near Eastern Studies, I acquired a new hobby. I hadn't planned on it. I certainly didn't need it and probably couldn't afford it. Yet I couldn't help myself. Isn't that what they say about any hobby—whether it is gardening or golf, photography or painting, scrapbooking or shoe shopping? I became an antiquities collector. Israel is one of the few places left in the world where you can legally purchase antiquities—ceramic pots and bowls, lamps, Roman glassware, coins, jewelry, and even ancient weaponry. One of my colleagues, an experienced archaeologist, introduced me to antiquities and taught me all about the characteristics of artifacts from the various time periods, as well as how to recognize genuine antiquities from modern fabrications. To me, it is amazing to hold items in my hands that are thousands of years old—genuine objects that belonged to and were used by real-life people who may have lived at

the time of Father Abraham or witnessed the miracles of Jesus of Nazareth. Over the years I have collected several different pieces, but I am particularly drawn to oil lamps. I have ancient oil lamps from the times of the Old Testament patriarchs, such as Abraham and Isaac, as well as from the time periods associated with King David and the prophets Jeremiah and Lehi. There are some from Greek and Roman times and some from the Byzantine and early Islamic period. But my favorite is a small oil lamp that dates to the time of the Savior.

This Herodian-style lamp fits in the palm of my hand. It is my favorite not because it is the oldest, most ornate, or of greatest monetary value, but rather because of what it represents to me. It is my favorite because of its *proximity to Jesus,* not because of *where* it came from or *when* it was used, but rather, because it represents something Jesus taught that has particular relevance and meaning to me in my life right here and now. I call it my "ten virgins lamp." This little oil lamp

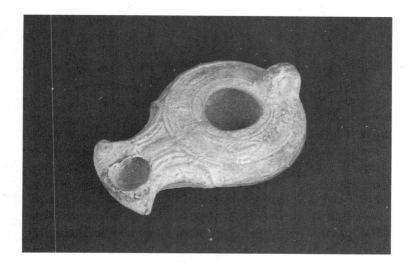

from the time of Jesus is the inspiration for this book. Different from the other ancient pieces in my collection that speak to me of a historical past, this "ten virgins lamp" powerfully speaks to me of the preparatory present and the prophetic future.

The parable of the ten virgins, recorded in Matthew 25, has been called "a special warning" associated with the Savior's Second Coming and specifically addressed to members of The Church of Jesus Christ of Latter-day Saints.[1] And whenever the phrase *Second Coming* pops up in sacrament meeting talks or lessons in classes and quorums, our minds usually go to "signs of the times"—prophesied events that must occur prior to the glorious return of the Son of God. Through the years of my career as a religious educator, I have probably had more questions asked by students concerning the "end times" than about any other doctrine in the scriptures. There seems to be a fascination with, almost a fixation on, apocalyptic prophecies and trying to establish some sort of timeline for events leading up to the Second Coming and Millennium. That is, however, *not* the focus of this book. Others have written and will continue to write about the "signs of the times" and their meanings. This book is more about *preparation* than *prophecy*—more about *spiritual readiness* than *sign recognition*. That's what my little oil lamp speaks to me.

The chapters that follow are organized into four main sections: "The Question," "The Answer," "The Meaning," and "The Promise." In teaching His disciples, both anciently and in modern times, Jesus addressed their (and our) questions: "When will you come again?" "What are the signs that will precede that event?" "Will it be in our generation?" "Will I be alive when you come?" In response to these kinds of questions, Jesus has repeatedly given "The Answer." Some of the chapters will directly address the answers Jesus has given. Most of the book, however, will address "The Meaning" behind or application of those answers—what the Savior wants us to take away from the content and methodology of His teachings on the subject. The final section, "The Promise," discusses the Savior's promises to the world concerning His glorious return—promises that are both universal and individual, glorious promises for the righteous and dreadful for the wicked.

Perhaps you, like I, have had classes in years past where we "crammed" our brains full of information in preparation for the final exam. We worried about knowing the right answers for the test and getting a good grade in the course. I would venture to guess that you have had similar experiences to mine—forgetting the answers shortly after the exam is over and quickly flushing much of the information that I crammed into my head throughout the semester. In contrast, those classes and learning experiences that have had the most enduring impact on my life were those that helped me to perceive the meaning behind the answers—to make relevant connections to my life and to inspire me to be a better person. That is my hope for you as you read this book. I hope you will find it *interesting* as we explore the answers, but, more important, *inspiring* as we find personal meaning in the Savior's words and comfort and courage in His promises.

My ultimate objective with this book is to help infuse greater hope into your heart and mind as you look to the future—both the great and the dreadful things that are associated with the last days and the Savior's Second Coming. It is my desire that you and I, and our families and those we love and serve, can all be filled with peace and joy even during the darkest and most difficult times. I have always been impressed that the righteous, faithful peoples of the Book of Mormon found happiness and prospered in the Lord even in times of war, bloodshed, persecution, and a society ruled by corrupt leaders and secret combinations. Of course, there were concerns and apprehension, as well as sorrow and suffering, but their faith in the fulfillment of the Lord's promises and peaceable riches of the companionship of the Holy Spirit gave them strength. As President Thomas S. Monson reminded us: "Though the storm clouds may gather, though the rains may pour down upon us, our knowledge of the gospel and our love of our Heavenly Father and of our Savior will comfort and sustain us and bring joy to our hearts as we walk uprightly and keep the commandments. There will be nothing in this world that can defeat us." He concluded, "Be of good cheer. The future is as bright as your faith."[2]

Now a disclaimer or two:

The fact that this book does not focus primarily on signs and prophecies does *not* mean that I am dismissing or disbelieving them. I have studied the "signs of the times" a great deal. I, like you, have grappled with how to understand them in the context of the scriptures and to make meaning of them in my life. I am not sure I have all (or many) of the answers to my questions. But what I do know for sure is that I love the scriptures and teachings of latter-day prophets and apostles. Both personally and professionally, I have spent a lifetime studying and teaching them. This book, although not a comprehensive examination of the "signs of the times" and issues surrounding the topic of the Second Coming, is my sincere attempt to promote spiritual readiness—"drop by drop in righteous living"[3]—regardless of what is happening in the world around us or when that "great and dreadful day" of His coming will inevitably occur.

Although I have sought earnestly for that which I have written to be in harmony with and supportive of the doctrine and teachings of the Church and its leaders, I alone am responsible for the conclusions drawn and opinions expressed. This is my own work and should not be viewed as an official publication of either The Church of Jesus Christ of Latter-day Saints or Brigham Young University. I do hope, however, that what I have written will reflect well on both institutions that I love so deeply.

Part 1

THE QUESTION

"I WONDER WHEN HE COMES AGAIN"

One of my favorite Primary songs when I was growing up was "When He Comes Again," by Mirla Greenwood Thayne. I think its lyrics capture the feelings we all share concerning the Second Coming.

> *I wonder, when he comes again,*
> *Will herald angels sing?*
> *Will earth be white with drifted snow,*
> *Or will the world know spring?*
> *I wonder if one star will shine*
> *Far brighter than the rest;*
> *Will daylight stay the whole night through?*
> *Will songbirds leave their nests?*
> *I'm sure he'll call his little ones*
> *Together round his knee,*
> *Because he said in days gone by,*
> *"Suffer them to come to me."*[4]

Wondering about the Lord's glorious coming and the signs

and wonders that will precede it is not just a modern phenomenon. "When will He come again?" is an age-old question. It has been on the minds and lips of believers for thousands of years.

Just days before He would be crucified, Jesus took the disciples to the Mount of Olives for an important teaching moment—the import of which they did not fully comprehend. With the magnificent temple as the backdrop, Jesus declared: "See ye not all these things? verily I say unto you, There shall not be left here one stone upon another, that shall not be thrown down" (Matthew 24:2). To say that the disciples "wondered" at the meaning of the Master's words would be an understatement. "Tell us, when shall these things be? And what shall be the sign of thy coming, and the end of the world?" (Matthew 24:3). Their questions reflect both confusion and conflation. "How can this temple that took forty years to build be so utterly destroyed that not one stone shall be left upon another?" One can only imagine their distress at the thought. No wonder they conflated two events into one—the destruction of the temple and of the city of Jerusalem must mean the "end of the world." It is completely understandable that they would link the two.

Only weeks later, on the very same mount, these disciples (minus Judas) would gaze with wonder at the resurrected Christ ascending into heaven and behold angels who declared, "This same Jesus, which is taken up from you into heaven, shall so come in like manner as ye have seen him go into heaven" (Acts 1:11). It would have been reasonable for these disciples to assume the Savior's return would be in the not-too-distant future—perhaps merely days, weeks, or months, or at tops a few years, but not centuries or millennia. Jesus hadn't told them otherwise. In fact, He had used the phrase "this generation shall not pass" until many of the prophesied events would be fulfilled (Matthew 24:34). He had given the signs, but not the schedule. Yet the hopes and expectations of the Apostles would be conveyed to the Church in their teachings and testimonies of Christ's eventual return. They were eye- and ear-witnesses of His Ascension and were instructed that He would return. No wonder so many of the first-century Christians likewise expected an imminent Second Coming. In response to this growing sentiment, the Apostle Paul rebuked the Thessalonian Saints who were "shaken in mind . . . that the day of Christ is at hand." Paul admonished, "Let no man deceive you by any means, for that day shall not come, except there come a falling away first, and that man of sin be revealed, the son of perdition" (2 Thessalonians 2:2–3; see also 1 Thessalonians 5).

Despite apostolic warnings like these and repeated admonishments to avoid becoming caught up with Second Coming sensationalism and apocalyptic alarm, there have been many in every generation that assume the answer to the age-old question "When will He come again?" is "Now." It is understandable. Signs appear before our eyes like leaves on the summer fig tree (see Matthew 24:32–33). Prophecies seem to be fulfilled. It is quite natural to assume that the day has arrived. It has been so in every generation. Like the illusive mirage on a hot highway—always appearing before us, but always beyond our reach—the signs of the Second Coming are ever before our eyes. That is both a blessing and a curse.

> *One who believes in a second coming of Christ that will usher in a millennial reign . . . has special challenges in reading signs. First, he is urged to notice lest he be caught unawares. Second, he must be aware of how many false readings and alarms there have been in bygone days, even by the faithful. . . . Our task is to react and to notice without overreacting. . . . [We are] to ponder signs without becoming paranoid, to be aware without frantically matching current events with scriptural expectations.*
>
> —Neal A. Maxwell, *"For the Power Is in Them . . ."* (1970), 20

Even in our dispensation, faithful members of the Church of the nineteenth century believed and some leaders taught that the Savior's return would be within a few years or decades. With all of the prophecies and revelations contained in the Doctrine and Covenants concerning the establishment of Zion, the temple in the New Jerusalem, the great council at Adam-ondi-Ahman, and the glorious return of Christ foremost in their minds, many Latter-day Saints—both prominent leaders and rank-and-file members—often spoke of and planned on the imminence of the Second Coming. Let me share just a few examples. In an interview in 1870, David Whitmer, one of the Three Witnesses of the Book of Mormon, said that the Prophet Joseph had taught that the New Jerusalem would be built in preparation for the Second Coming before the Three Witnesses died. As a result, Whitmer was convinced that the remarkable events associated with the "end times" were "right around the corner." Brigham Young likewise shared his own opinion that the building of the temple in the New Jerusalem would be done before the building of the Salt Lake Temple.[5] He told people that it could occur in as few as seven years. On more than one occasion, Wilford Woodruff surmised that the Second Coming would occur before the turn of the century.[6] These predictions are but a few of many similar pronouncements that reflected the prevailing opinion that those Saints would witness the Second Coming in their lifetimes.

"I have asked frequently when is that time coming, which I have heard talked about and prophesied of in tongues years ago when in the meetings of the Saints," said Elder Joseph A. Young, brother of President Brigham Young and longtime senior president of the First Council of the Seventy. "I have heard men prophesy in the early part of this Church, that in 25 years Jesus would come to reign upon the earth, and that in that time all would be wound up." We can understand that they, like us, desperately wanted to know the answer to the *when* question. Yet, we are left to wonder why their predictions were so far off. Were the predictions just wishful thinking, overzealous speculations common to the culture of that day, or innocent but faithful expressions of a personal opinion? Or is it possible that they were indeed inspired by the Lord in some manner, but their mortal comprehension and interpretations were insufficient? Elder Joseph Young explained that many Saints in the nineteenth century (and we could apply the same principle by extension to ancient disciples and Christians throughout the millennia) misconstrued and miscalculated on a number of matters because they were so excited to fulfill the prophecies. As a result, they could not fully comprehend or accept the Lord's divine timetable. Things "appeared" to be closer in mortal minds than in God's. Paraphrasing what God said to Isaiah, "My ways are not your ways and my reckoning of time is not your reckoning of time" (see Isaiah 55:8–9). "The Holy Spirit brought many things close to their minds—they appeared right by, and hence many were deceived, and run into a mistake respecting them," Elder Young explained. ". . . I knew that faith and the Holy Ghost brought the designs of Providence close by, and by that means we were enabled to scan them, and find out what they would produce when carried into effect, *but we had not knowledge enough to digest and fully comprehend those things.*"[7] Without God's infinite view of time and eternity, it becomes easy to conflate and compact the "signs of the times" in ways that make things appear, at least to mortal minds, much closer than they really may be. This resulted in what Elder Joseph Young called "the folly of making great calculations beforehand."

Just as men in centuries past have tried to predict the end of the world and the Second Coming, we see many in our day who do the same. Even in my lifetime I have seen numerous examples—some humorous, bordering on crazy; some serious, resulting in tragic consequences. It seems that with every major natural calamity, political upheaval, war, or economic collapse in the world, there are many who declare the end near. "This is it." "Armageddon." "End of the world." Because the prophecies concerning the last days, such as the destruction of the wicked at Christ's Second Coming and the millennial reign of the King of kings, are a significant part of our theology, it is not unreasonable to "wonder when He comes again." Like the disciples in Jesus's day, we have been told to watch and be ready (see Matthew 24:42–44). We know the signs. We see them around us. Of course, we wonder and want to know when. Unfortunately, I have seen how the innocent "wondering" described in the familiar Primary song, if not guarded against, can swell to fruitless speculation that dangerously distracts individuals from their spiritual missions—their more proximate duties and need for continual faithfulness—or creates an unhealthy anxiety that destroys faith and engenders fear.

When I began my teaching career many years ago, it was customary to begin seminary classes with a brief devotional conducted by the students. Most of the time these devotionals were nice but not necessarily profound or remarkable. Once in a while, however, a student would deliver a memorable spiritual thought that would really stick with the class. One such time was when a young man who typically didn't say much and rarely, if ever, had participated in class presented the devotional. His father had shared with him something he had received in his high priests group the previous Sunday. The father was excited to share it with his family. The son found it so exciting that he wanted everyone in his seminary class to have a copy of it.

We had been studying the New Testament in seminary that year, and so this student made the necessary connection between his spiritual thought and what we had studied. "Jesus said nobody knows when the Second Coming will be," this young man stated. "That may have been true in Jesus's day, but *now we know.*" Boy, that got my attention! He then distributed a handout to each member of the class and went through it point by point. I don't remember everything he said, but I do remember that it offered someone's calculations based on scriptural prophecies (or at least the author's interpretations of scripture), astronomy, tradition (or what could be characterized as Mormon folklore), and the "prophecies" of the sixteenth-century "seer" Nostradamus. According to the person who had compiled the "signs" and made the prediction, the Second Coming would occur on a Sunday, that it must be an Easter Sunday, and that it must fall on April 6th. It would come when all of the planets in our solar system were "lined up," and it must be exactly six thousand years after the Fall of Adam. Many of these calculations and signs were so unbelievable they were laughable, and I almost did laugh out loud as the student read through the handout. I thought he was joking, but I could see that he was dead serious, and his classmates were very interested.

The bottom line resulting from all these speculations was that the Second Coming would occur on April 6, 1996—which seemed a long time away at that moment. The students were excited by what they had heard and could talk of nothing else the rest of the class. It was not long until this handout was copied and circulated in various quorums and classes in many wards and stakes. It spread like wildfire throughout the entire area.

April 6, 1996, has come and gone, and we have not witnessed the Second Coming (as far as I know). Yet, over the years, I have continued to come across similar calculations and attempts to nail down the exact date of the coming of the Lord. "We may not know the day or the hour," some have said, "but we can know the year." Political events on the world stage, popular movies or books, or someone's reported visions or spiritual experiences always generate some degree of sensational speculation and what I call "Second Coming anxiety." For example, at the outbreak of the Gulf War in 1991 (and subsequent wars in the region since) I heard members of the Church speculate that it was the commencement of the battle of Armageddon. With the close of 1999 and the dawn of the new millennium came all kinds of concerns and speculation. The year 2000 seemed to hold some mystical power in the minds of many, perhaps because of their interpretation of the "seven seals" prophecy of John the Revelator. There was talk of the impending "rapture" among many Christians. In fact, some were so convinced that they sold their homes and property, gave away all their possessions, and then went to hilltops to wait—but nothing happened. Then there was the Mayan calendar craze that supposedly established 2012 as the year, December the month, and the 21st the day. That has come and gone, but I have seen "revisions" explaining that they misread the calendar and 2015 was the "real date." But that year has also come and gone.

There was a massive Indian Ocean tsunami in 2004 that took hundreds of thousands of lives, the devastation of Hurricane Katrina in 2005, the stock market crash of 2008, and the real-estate bubble burst of 2014 that left individuals and institutions in financial ruin. Each of these cataclysmic events caused many to feel that the end of the world was indeed imminent. Recently, there was a "blood moon"—a once-in-a-generation astronomical event that combined a full lunar eclipse with the proximity of the moon being at its closest to the earth, producing a unique bloodred color. I had heard so much about this event being the sign of the end of the world that I secretly hoped I would not need to set my alarm for the next morning. But the sun came up as usual, and I had to go to work.

> *Can we use . . . scientific data to extrapolate that the Second Coming is likely to occur during the next few years, or the next decade, or the next century? Not really. I am called as one of the apostles to be a special witness of Christ in these exciting, trying times, and I do not know when He is going to come again. As far as I know, none of my brethren in the Council of the Twelve or even in the First Presidency know. And I would humbly suggest to you . . . that if we do not know, then nobody knows, no matter how compelling their arguments or how reasonable their calculations.*
>
> —M. Russell Ballard, "When Shall These Things Be?" BYU Devotional, March 12, 1996

Another "researcher" recently received national and international attention by predicting the apocalypse would occur on Saturday, September 23, 2017. When that date came and went, he altered his prediction by saying that the terrible flooding and devastation accompanying Hurricanes Harvey, Irma, and Maria was just the beginning, and the end of the world was just around the corner. He cited the "signs of the times" coupled with symbolic numbers found in the Bible, particularly the book of Revelation, as "proof" that the destruction of the world and the Second Coming would happen in 2018. What do you think? Is that possible? Probable?

We all wonder and wait and look forward to His coming. We, like the Savior's ancient disciples, want to know when that day will be. "I don't know when the Savior will come. I'm ready for Him. I hope it isn't too long in this evil-filled world," President Gordon B. Hinckley taught. "I don't know. Neither do the angels in heaven. None of us knows."[8] Although we may wonder, "When will He come again?," we must remember that neither science, signs, nor speculation can adequately answer that age-old question. Only the Savior Himself can provide the answer. Let us now examine the answers found in holy writ.

Part 2

THE ANSWER

Chapter 2

"TROUBLE ME NO MORE ON THIS MATTER"

Tell us, when shall these things be?" the ancient disciples asked the Savior, "and what shall be the sign of thy coming, and of the end of the world?" (Matthew 24:3). Jesus answered their question by enumerating many signs and wonders that would precede His wondrous return. The Joseph Smith Translation of Matthew chapter 24 is found in the Pearl of Great Price as Joseph Smith—Matthew (JS—M). It more clearly organizes the signs with the corresponding events about which the disciples asked—the destruction of Jerusalem and Herod's temple, and the Second Coming of Christ and the "end of the world." The Savior's teachings found in Matthew 24 are further clarified in a revelation given to the Prophet Joseph Smith that is recorded in Doctrine and Covenants, section 45. "I will show it plainly as I showed it unto my disciples as I stood before them in the flesh, and spake unto them," the Lord declared as preface to His modern answer to the nearly two-thousand-year-old question (D&C 45:16). These three scriptural sources list the signs given by the Savior, but they are not the only signs given by Him. Numerous signs are found throughout the standard works. Other "signs and wonders" are also found in the prophetic teachings of apostles and prophets of this last dispensation. They could not be adequately discussed in a whole library of books. It is not my intent in this book to focus much on signs other than to give this brief "snapshot" of what Jesus taught His disciples and to show the context for His answers to their question. This brief list is not comprehensive or exhaustive, and it is certainly not sequential.[9]

- "False Christs and false prophets" will show "great signs and wonders" that, if possible, "shall deceive the very elect, who are the elect according to the covenant" (Matthew 24:24; Mark 13:22; JS—M 1:21–22).
- "Wars, and rumors of wars"; the "abomination of desolation" (D&C 45:26; 87:1–6; JS—M 1:23, 28–29, 32).
- The whole earth shall be in commotion (see D&C 88:91).
- "Iniquity shall abound, the love of men shall wax cold"; the wicked shall turn their hearts from God "because of the precepts of men" (D&C 45:27–29; JS—M 1:30).
- "Men's hearts shall fail them"; "fear shall come upon all people" (D&C 63:33; 88:91).
- Signs in the heavens and earth; blood, fire, vapors of smoke, "the sun shall be darkened, and the moon shall not give her light"; "stars shall fall from heaven" (D&C 29:14; 45:39–42; JS—M 1:33).
- Famines, pestilences, hailstorms that destroy crops; overflowing scourges and sicknesses; flies and maggots

will eat flesh from bones; eyes will fall from their sockets; earthquakes, desolations, and calamities in divers places (see D&C 29:16–20; 43:25; 45:31–33; 88:87–90; JS—M 1:29).

- Restoration of the gospel; gospel preached in all the world; Church growth and strength throughout the world; temples dotting the earth (see D&C 133:37–38; JS—M 1:26, 31).

- Scattering and gathering of Israel; remnant of believing Jews gathered to Jerusalem; wicked shall be "bound in bundles" and destroyed; "Zion shall flourish" and "disciples shall stand in holy places"; "Lamanites shall blossom as the rose" (D&C 29:9; 45:32, 43–44; 49:24–25; 101:16–23, 66; JS—M 1:27).

- Establishment of the New Jerusalem (see 3 Nephi 20:22; Ether 13:2–6; D&C 45:66–69).

- The "sign of the Son of Man" shall appear in the heavens and "all the tribes of the earth [shall] mourn" (JS—M 1:36).

By giving these signs as directly and specifically as He did, the Savior answered the question of the disciples, both ancient and modern. Yet He didn't really answer their question—at least the way they (and we) wanted it answered. No matter how many signs He cited, no matter how much He or others have commented on the given signs, the answer does not satisfy without sequential specificity. "Inquiring minds want to know" not just the signs, but the dates! But it doesn't work that way—at least not now.

> *It is not possible for us, in our present relatively low state of spiritual understanding, to specify the exact chronology of all the events that shall attend the Second Coming. Nearly all of the prophetic word relative to our Lord's return links various events together without reference to the order of their occurrence. Indeed, the same scriptural language is often used to describe similar events that will take place at different times.*
>
> —Bruce R. McConkie, *The Millennial Messiah* (1982), 635

As I have thought about why we don't always "get it" when it comes to signs and sequence, a parallel comes to mind—a parallel to which almost every parent or grandparent who has ever traveled with small children can relate. "How much farther, Daddy?" "Are we there yet?" "When will we be there?" "Is that it?" I have heard those questions and myriads more like them more times than I care to remember. I learned as a father (and experienced as a child but didn't fully understand) that no answer—no matter how specific or precise—can adequately satisfy the child. I don't think, for example, that a three-year-old could comprehend and quit asking, "How much farther?" if I were to say, "We have one thousand and eighty-seven miles until we arrive at Disneyland." Even answers like, "We'll be there in an hour" (or even fifteen minutes) can't satisfy a child who doesn't fully fathom time or distance, whose excitement is unbounded, and whose attention span is slightly less than a nanosecond.

In a way, we are like children. Answers have been given,

but they don't satisfy us because we cannot comprehend the Lord's Second Coming timetable any better than little children can understand hours and minutes, miles and landmarks, or signals and road signs along the highway. In fact, the Second Coming to us will be much like going to Disneyland is for little children—we may see some advertising signs along the way, but we won't know the timing for sure until we arrive. Thus our patient Father answers over and over again, "Soon."

In His discourse to the disciples on the Mount of Olives (and in modern-day revelations found in the Doctrine and Covenants), the Savior answered their questions about signs, but He gave one answer to them that matters most of all. In fact, He repeated it again and again for emphasis. You can see this answer "bracketing," as it were—almost like bookends—His teachings on signs. It is almost as if the Savior is pleading with the disciples not to become distracted from His real message by overly focusing on signs. You can almost hear the Master saying, "As you look for these signs and see them fulfilled, remember that no man knows when the Second Coming is, so be ready always." He uses phrases like:

- "Take heed that no man deceive you" (Matthew 24:4).
- "But of that day and hour knoweth no man, no, not the angels of heaven, but my Father only" (Matthew 24:36).
- "Watch therefore: for ye know not what hour your Lord doth come" (Matthew 24:42).
- "Therefore be ye also ready: for in such an hour as ye think not the Son of man cometh" (Matthew 24:44).
- "Take ye heed, watch and pray: for ye know not when the time is" (Mark 13:33).

In this dispensation, the Lord has reiterated that message and provided additional insight and emphasis. In calling early missionaries to "declare [His] gospel unto a crooked and perverse generation," the Savior taught that "the field is white already to harvest; and *it is the eleventh hour,* and the *last time* that I shall call laborers into my vineyard" (D&C 33:2–3; emphasis added). Speaking specifically regarding the calls of Ezra Thayre and Northrop Sweet, but by extension and application to all latter-day missionaries and disciples, He declared: "Wherefore, thrust in your sickles, and reap with all your might, mind, and strength. . . . Open your mouths and spare not, . . . for behold, verily, verily, I say unto you, that *I come quickly*" (D&C 33:7, 9, 18; emphasis added). Only weeks later, the Lord through the Prophet Joseph Smith called Orson Pratt to "lift up your voice as with the sound of a trump, both long and loud, and cry repentance unto a crooked and perverse generation, preparing the way of the Lord for his second coming." Again, the Savior said, *"I come quickly,"* adding to His previous declaration that *"the time is soon at hand* that I shall come in a cloud with power and great glory" (D&C 34:6–7, 12; emphasis added). Thirteen times in the Doctrine and Covenants, the Lord states, in one form or another, "I come quickly." He describes His Second Coming as being "nigh at hand" another twelve times and as "soon" six times. The resurrected Lord Himself declared that His coming is "near, even at the doors" (D&C 110:16). And that was in 1836! So I think we can safely surmise that the "great and dreadful day of the Lord" is "nigher at hand" and "sooner" than ever before! If it was "near, even at the doors" in 1836, we can assume that it is much nearer now—perhaps even knocking, pounding, or breaking the door down. Yet, despite all this, Christ clearly taught, both in the meridian of time and in the fulness of times, that no one knows exactly when that great event will occur. "For the time is at hand," He declared in 1831, "*the day or the hour no man knoweth;* but it surely shall come" (D&C 39:21; emphasis added; see also D&C 51:20; 61:38; 124:10; 133:11).

Nothing illustrates this better, in my estimation, than an experience in the life of the Prophet Joseph Smith. He recounted this experience in 1843, although it had occurred years earlier.

"I was once praying very earnestly to know the time of the coming of the Son of Man, when I heard a voice repeat the following:

"Joseph, my son, if thou livest until thou art eighty-five years old, thou shalt see the face of the Son of Man; therefore *let this suffice, and trouble me no more on this matter.*

"I was left thus, without being able to decide whether this coming referred to the beginning of the millennium or to some previous appearing, or whether I should die and thus see his face.

"I believe the coming of the Son of Man will not be any sooner than that time" (D&C 130:14–17; emphasis added).

What did the Lord mean by that? Didn't an omniscient God know when Joseph would die? Of course He did! Then why this riddle? Was the Lord toying with the Prophet in some way? I don't know about that, but I am confident that cosmic pranks are not among the works of the Almighty. I believe the Master Teacher was utilizing a unique teaching technique to get Joseph really thinking about what he was asking the Lord (which he certainly did). Rather than giving a direct answer, the Lord seemed to be helping Joseph answer his own question. I believe He was leading the Prophet to an understanding that knowing *when* the Second Coming will occur isn't as critical to life and salvation as knowing other things. I can almost hear the Savior saying, "Can't you see that I have already given you the answer to your question? Let that suffice. Don't worry so much about it! You have more important things that should occupy your attention and devotion. So don't bother me anymore about an exact date. I've told you all I will right now. Now, go about doing what you are supposed to be doing."

That's the way I imagine it, because all parents know that sometimes their children ask the same question over and over again even though they have already answered it—over and over again. "There's nothing more to talk about" is a parental phrase that usually drives children, particularly teens, crazy. For a parent, it means, "I've already said everything that needs to be said about this subject. You know my answer. The matter is settled. The decision is made. Move on." Unfortunately, for the child it rarely settles the matter. Often the child's response conveys the feeling, "I know what you said, but I don't like the answer."

It is much the same way for us today as we "wonder when He comes again." Like children, we don't know the meaning of all things. We usually want more rather than less, and often we fail to perceive the real message behind the answers we have been given. We hear what we want to hear instead of what we should have heard. We can't see very far down the road. The

Lord's injunction to Joseph Smith may apply to each of us as we consider the signs of the times and the Second Coming of Christ: "Let this suffice." "Trouble me no more on this matter." The answers He has given are sufficient.

In the discourse to His disciples given on the Mount of Olives shortly before His death, Jesus specifically said "no man knoweth" four separate times. What part of that don't we understand? We need not persist in asking "When?" We need not be troubled as we see the signs fulfilled before our very eyes. He has assured us that He will indeed return in glory. That is not in question. Though we must not "trouble" the Lord on the matter of *when*, we can know that He has answered it—over and over again. He invites us to move forward in righteous readiness and prepare to meet Him whenever that day comes.

Chapter 3

"HE HATH ALREADY COME"

Luke's account of Jesus's discourse given on the Mount of Olives shortly before His death—the discourse in which He taught the disciples concerning the signs of the last days and the end of the world—contains an important parable, although it is lesser known than the Savior's other parables of preparation for the Second Coming. Like the more familiar parable of the ten virgins, this lesser-known parable is intended to teach disciples, both ancient and modern, to be watchful, prayerful, and ever prepared. In the parable, Jesus likens the disciples to servants who have the responsibility to watch over the household (the Church) while the master (Christ) attends a wedding feast (ascends to heaven). They have their assigned tasks, and if they are found faithful when the master returns they will be invited to join him at a final feast (inherit celestial glory). The Joseph Smith Translation of these verses provides us with an important insight—the Savior's coming, as it were, comes at different times to different people.

"For, behold, he cometh in the first watch of the night, and he shall also come in the second watch, and again he shall come in the third watch.

"And verily I say unto you, He hath already come, as it is written of him; and again when he shall come in the second watch, or come in the third watch, blessed are those servants when he cometh, that he shall find so doing;

"For the Lord of those servants shall gird himself, and make them to sit down to meat, and will come forth and serve them.

"And now, verily I say these things unto you, that ye may know this, that the coming of the Lord is as a thief in the night. . . .

"And he said unto them, Verily I say unto you, be ye therefore ready also; for the Son of Man cometh at an hour when ye think not" (JST, Luke 12:41–44, 47; emphasis added).

The ancient Roman day was generally divided into twelve hours of light and twelve hours of darkness. Night was divided into four watches of three hours each because it was generally accepted that a city guard could not watch effectively all night. So there would be a changing of the guards every three hours. The fourth watch was the three-hour period right before sunrise. So what does Jesus mean by the phrase "he cometh in the first watch of the night," the second watch, the third, and so on? How is it possible that "he hath already come"? What is the Lord trying to teach us today with this parable?

Jesus purposely identifies all four watches of the night as times in which the master returns. There is not just one time when he returns to check on the servants and to receive an accounting of their labors in the master's household. Two important messages are apparent: (1) you don't know when *your* "day of reckoning" will come, so (2) be ready to meet the Master at any time.

> *All of the Lord's ministers, all of the members of his Church, and for that matter all men everywhere ("What I say unto one, I say unto all"), are counseled to await with righteous readiness the coming of the Lord. However, most men will die before he comes, and only those then living will rejoice or tremble, as the case may be, at his personal presence. But all who did prepare will be rewarded as though they had lived when he came, while the wicked will be "cut asunder" and appointed their "portion with the hypocrites" as surely as though they lived in the very day of dread and vengeance.*
>
> *Thus, in effect, the Lord comes in every watch of the night, on every occasion when men are called to face death and judgment.*
>
> —Bruce R. McConkie, *Doctrinal New Testament Commentary,* 3 vols. (1965–1973), 1:676–77

Each of us will face our own Second Coming of Christ, so to speak, whether at the moment we die or when the Savior comes in glory to usher in the Millennium. In the Doctrine and Covenants, the Lord uses language similar to that in the New Testament parables. "Hearken unto my voice *lest death shall overtake you; in an hour when ye think not* the summer shall be past, and the harvest ended, and your souls not saved" (D&C 45:2; emphasis added). It is clear from both ancient and modern scripture that what the Lord wants us to understand concerning the *when* of the Second Coming is this: Knowing the date or seeing the signs means little compared to being spiritually prepared. Likewise, life or death does not determine the greatness or dreadfulness of that day. It is our righteousness or wickedness that matters most. Every day is potentially a "day of reckoning" for God's children. Only a tiny portion of the world's population will be alive at the Lord's glorious return. For the billions and billions who are not alive at that day, they will have experienced a preliminary Second Coming, so to speak, when they die. Some will have died in the "first watch"—the early days of world history. Others will leave mortality in subsequent seasons—in every "watch of the night." They will experience, to some degree and in some manner, the "great and dreadful day of the Lord" *as if* they were on earth when He comes again.

As I have taught this concept of "righteous readiness," as Elder Bruce R. McConkie called it, and shared these scriptures with my own students at BYU through the years, I have posed a follow-up question: "Now, in light of all this, do you want to know the exact day when the Savior will come?" The students usually shake their heads no and say, "We don't know the exact day"—demonstrating that they have heard loud and clear and understood what I have been teaching them. Then I push them a little more. "I'm serious," I say. "I can tell you the exact day." They push back. "No, you can't. You've just been telling us that no one knows." To which I respond, "Oh, yes, I can. And I will show you in the scriptures. You can go home and call your parents. You can tell your roommates. You can post it on social media. You can write it in your journal. You can 'take it to the bank,' so to speak. I can tell you the exact day!" That gets their attention (even though some laugh and think I am joking)! Then we turn to the sixty-fourth section of the Doctrine and Covenants and read the Lord's own words.

> *What if the day of His coming were tomorrow? If we knew that we would meet the Lord tomorrow—through our premature death or through His unexpected coming—what would we do today? What confessions would we make? What practices would we discontinue? What accounts would we settle? What forgivenesses would we extend? What testimonies would we bear?*
>
> *If we would do those things then, why not now? Why not seek peace while peace can be obtained? If our lamps of preparation are drawn down, let us start immediately to replenish them.*
>
> —Dallin H. Oaks, "Preparation for the Second Coming," *Ensign*, May 2004, 9

"Behold, now *it is called today until the coming of the Son of Man,* and verily it is a day of sacrifice, and a day for the tithing of my people; for he that is tithed shall not be burned at his coming.

"For after today cometh the burning—this is speaking after the manner of the Lord—for verily I say, *tomorrow all the proud and they that do wickedly shall be as stubble;* and I will burn them up, for I am the Lord of Hosts; and I will not spare any that remain in Babylon" (D&C 64:23–24; emphasis added).

> *Certainly there is no point in speculating concerning the day and the hour. Let us rather live each day so that if the Lord does come while we are yet upon the earth we shall be worthy of that change which will occur as in the twinkling of an eye and under which we shall be changed from mortal to immortal beings. And if we should die before he comes, then—if our lives have conformed to his teachings—we shall arise in that resurrection morning and be partakers of the marvelous experiences designed for those who shall live and work with the Savior in that promised Millennium. We need not fear the day of his coming; the very purpose of the Church is to provide incentive and the opportunity for us to conduct our lives in such a way that those who are members of the kingdom of God will become members of the kingdom of heaven when he establishes that kingdom on the earth.*
>
> —Gordon B. Hinckley, *Teachings of Gordon B. Hinckley* (1997), 576

"When will the Lord come?" I ask again. "What is the exact day (notice I didn't say date)?" They all respond, "Tomorrow."

That is the right answer—straight from the mouth of the Lord Himself. We can rest assured that the Lord will indeed come *tomorrow*—whenever that is—whether in the first watch or second watch or later. Tomorrow we will greet the Lord—whether in the body or out. Tomorrow will come, but *today* we need to be preparing and worthy—all day, each day, every day—no matter how long today may be. Well, since we now know *when* the Second Coming will be—tomorrow—let us devote ourselves to the greater issue of *what*—what we must do to be in "righteous readiness," to be spiritually prepared *today.*

Part 3

THE MEANING

Chapter 4

PARABLES OF PREPARATION

Throughout His ministry, Jesus used parables to teach important concepts, clarify sometimes difficult-to-understand doctrines, and call people to repentance. Jesus was not alone in using this teaching technique. Prophets in the Old Testament had used parables, and great teachers and rabbis of Jesus's day did likewise. Parables provided analogies and object lessons that would stick in the minds of the people because they were easily visualized and remembered. Such simple comparisons stimulated deeper thinking about complex principles. A parable took a common or mortal object and likened it to sacred, eternal principles. (The Greek word from which the modern English word *parable* is translated is *parabole,* and it literally means "to set side by side.") Likewise, parables allowed the Master to teach in such a way that listeners could "hear" things at different levels. For those with the Spirit, there was profound meaning, but for those who were not spiritually attuned, the parable was just a simple story. In this manner,

Jesus's parables both concealed and revealed the true meaning behind His teaching—*concealing* from those who would not have ears to hear or eyes to see, while *revealing* to those who by their faith in the Lord and by the power of the Spirit could comprehend what Jesus intended to convey (see Matthew 13:12–17).

As the Master Teacher, Jesus employed many different kinds of parables. Some were sophisticated stories with complex characters and plot, like the parable of the good Samaritan (see Luke 10). Others were just a few words of comparison, such as "the kingdom of heaven is like unto treasure hid in a field" (Matthew 13:44) or "I am the bread of life" (John 6:35) or the camel not being able to pass through the eye of the needle (see Matthew 19:24). Peppered throughout His teachings are all kinds of comparisons or parables that "set side by side" temporal objects with spiritual principles. There are metaphors, allegories, similes, and hyperbole—each serving to clearly illustrate eternal verities that may be purposely veiled from mortal view or fully comprehended by finite minds.

Such is certainly the case in the Savior's teachings concerning the signs of the last days and His Second Coming. "But of that day and hour knoweth no man, no, not the angels of heaven, but my Father only," Jesus declared (Matthew 24:36). The Savior used the parable of the fig tree to illustrate His point that although no mortal man knows when that day will be, all should be observant of the prophesied signs.

"Now learn a parable of the fig tree; When his branch is yet tender, and putteth forth leaves, ye know that summer is nigh:

"So likewise ye, when ye shall see all these things, know that it is near, even at the doors" (Matthew 24:32–33).

To illustrate His commandment to "watch therefore: for ye know not what hour your Lord doth come" (Matthew 24:42) and "be ye also ready: for in such an hour as ye think not the Son of man cometh" (Matthew 24:44), Jesus used comparisons that the disciples could readily understand. Likewise, many of the signs could be seen in virtually every subsequent generation. Lacking a specific timeline from Jesus Himself, you can see how the disciples may have been confused concerning when the prophecies would be fulfilled. The ambiguity seems purposeful. If these signs hadn't been given in a way that could be applied to every generation, then earlier generations may not have been as attentive to the signs; they may have slackened their efforts to hasten the work of salvation in their particular dispensation. Thus, it appears that the Savior is urging His followers in every generation to spend more time and energy on preparation than on calculation.

- His coming will be like the days of Noah when the flood caught people unprepared as they went about their life of "eating and drinking, marrying and giving in marriage" (Matthew 24:38). They paid no attention to the incessant warnings of Noah, his building of the ark, or the rainstorms until it was too late.
- The Second Coming will come so suddenly that, while working in the same field doing the same menial daily tasks, only one of the two laborers will be prepared to meet the Master. Likewise, only one person grinding grain at the mill will be ready, though another is nearby

engaged in her normal activities (see Matthew 24:40–41; Luke 17:34–36).

- The goodman of the house (the homeowner) should have been continually prepared to protect his property, because a thief doesn't schedule his home invasion (see Matthew 24:43).

- Servants who have been charged to watch always and protect the Master's belongings must not lazily assume the "lord delayeth his coming" and take time off to sleep or get drunk. Wise servants don't get distracted because they know "the lord of that servant shall come in a day when he looketh not for him, and in an hour that he is not aware of" (see Matthew 24:45–50).

Interestingly, Jesus's recitation of the signs that will precede the end of the world, the destruction of the wicked, and the Second Coming—given in response to the disciples' question—is recorded in only fifteen verses in Joseph Smith—Matthew. In contrast, the Savior's teachings concerning being continually watchful, ever spiritually prepared in righteous readiness, comprise nineteen verses in the very same chapter—and that doesn't even count the forty-six verses in the next chapter of Matthew (chapter 25) that contain what have come to be known as the "parables of preparation"—the ten virgins, the talents, and the sheep and goats. Just the difference in the number of verses in Jesus's discourse devoted to preparation as opposed to signs—more than a four-to-one ratio—should remind us where to focus our attention.

One of the rules of effective communication is to answer the question that should have been asked, not just the one that was asked. Jesus effectively used this principle on many occasions, answering questions but also teaching broader principles and giving counsel that His listeners needed to hear, even if they didn't ask for it. Perhaps the best example of this is the Savior's response to the disciples' questions concerning the Second Coming. When they asked, "When shall these things be? and what shall be the sign of thy coming?" (Matthew 24:3), the Savior answered but went further. There was more that they (and we) needed to hear but didn't ask. It is almost as if Jesus were saying, "I've answered your questions, but there is one that you didn't ask that is far more important: *What must we do to be prepared for that day?* The answer to that question is more important (even essential) than the answers I have already given you."

Similarly, in modern revelation, the Lord has given us even more specific information about the necessary preparations than He has about the prophetic signs of His coming. Both go hand in hand, but one (knowing the signs) may be *interesting,* even important, whereas the other (personal preparation) is *imperative.* How can we be ready and not be overtaken by spiritual slumber that will leave us unprepared and unworthy at His coming? Are we doing our part to further the work of the Lord and to be spiritually prepared to meet Him even if the Second Coming does not occur in our generation? That is the main emphasis of Jesus's teachings to the disciples on the Mount of Olives—*the meaning* of His answers to them and us today. Interestingly, He teaches them and answers their questions with three "parables of preparation."

The order in which these parables appear in Matthew,

chapter 25, is: first, the parable of the ten virgins; second, the parable of the talents; and last, the parable of the sheep and goats. Contextually, the parable of the ten virgins sets the stage for the other two parables, establishing the reason for the parables and teaching the need for continual preparation for the Savior's Second Coming. However, for my purposes in this chapter, I will discuss the parable of the ten virgins last as a transition to the rest of this book.

THE PARABLE OF THE TALENTS

Matthew 25:14–30

Probably every member of the Church and anyone who reads and loves the New Testament has heard sermons from the pulpit or lessons in classes citing the parable of the talents. Usually the underlying message of those talks or lessons is improving upon the gifts that God has given us. Although that certainly is an appropriate takeaway from the scriptural passage, the context of this parable—at least Matthew's account of Jesus's teachings to the disciples on the Mount of Olives shortly before His Crucifixion—actually deals more with preparation for the Second Coming and the great day of judgment than magnifying spiritual gifts (or financial investment strategies). Luke's parable of the pounds (see Luke, chapter 19) would fit better with the notion of spiritual enlargement, the development of gifts and abilities the Lord has given. A "talent," as used in these parables, is not to be confused with talents like musical or artistic ability. The talent of which Jesus is speaking is a monetary measurement, a coin used for wages and purchasing. There are many interpretations regarding the actual monetary value of a talent and its relationship to the other denominations of coins in Jesus's day. Whatever the "exchange rate," it is generally understood to be a significant sum, but that should not distract us from seeing the main point of the parable.

"For the kingdom of heaven is as a man travelling into a far country, who called his own servants, and delivered unto them his goods.

"And unto one he gave five talents, to another two, and to another one; to every man according to his several ability; and straightway to his journey" (Matthew 25:14–15).

The "man travelling into a far country" is Christ. After the Resurrection, He returns to His Father, promising to return at some future day to "his own servants." In preparation for His death and Ascension, He has given His earthly disciples all they need to govern the kingdom and to prepare for His return. To all of us is given the gift of His atoning sacrifice, but some have greater responsibilities, tasks, and even spiritual gifts. As disciples, we are instructed to use all of those gifts to serve the Lord and others and to prepare ourselves, our families, and our fellow men for the wrapping-up scenes of the last days of the world and the Final Judgment that will follow. That is when the "accounts" will be reckoned. "After a long time the lord of those servants cometh, and reckoneth with them" (Matthew 25:19).

I find it interesting that the amount of "increase" experienced by the man given five talents and the one given two doesn't seem to be significant, since both are granted the same reward for their faithfulness. "Well done, thou good and faithful servant," the lord said to both servants, "thou hast been faithful over a few things, I will make thee ruler over many things: enter thou into the joy of thy lord" (Matthew 25:21, 23). The man who was given one talent, by contrast, "hid [the] talent in the earth" because he was "afraid" (Matthew 25:25). To him, the returning lord declared that he was a "wicked and slothful servant," an "unprofitable servant" worthy of "outer darkness" with all its "weeping and gnashing of teeth" (Matthew 25:26, 30).

Principle of Preparedness
BE ANXIOUSLY ENGAGED

So what does this mean in the context of "waiting upon the Lord"—looking forward to and preparing for His return? To me, the message is that those who are "anxiously engaged" in doing the Lord's will, keeping their covenants, fulfilling their responsibilities—whether they are great or small—will be rewarded when the Master returns. On the other hand, those who are not "anxiously engaged" in faithful service to God and fellow man become like the man with only one talent who was "afraid," anxious, worried, panicked, paralyzed by fear. The curse came to him as a result of doing nothing. Likewise, we cannot faithfully "wait upon the Lord" and look forward to His coming, and at the same time be fretting and stewing about the signs of the times and sitting, so to speak, on the front porch with our bags packed, looking longingly to the sky, waiting to be lifted up.

Nearly thirty years ago, Bishop Glenn L. Pace, then in

the Presiding Bishopric of the Church, taught that faithful Latter-day Saints can best prepare for the Second Coming by reaching out to those in need, especially those who suffer amidst the long-prophesied calamities that will precede the great and dreadful day of the Lord. We cannot become, individually and institutionally, "the salt of the earth," Bishop Pace taught, "if we stay in one lump in the cultural halls of our beautiful meetinghouses."

He explained further: "We know the prophecies of the future. We know the final outcome. We know the world collectively will not repent and consequently the last days will be filled with much pain and suffering. Therefore, we could throw up our hands and do nothing but pray for the end to come so the millennial reign could begin. To do so would forfeit our right to participate in the grand event we are all awaiting. We must all become players in the winding-up scene, not spectators. We must do all we can to prevent calamities, and then do everything possible to assist and comfort the victims of tragedies that do occur."[10]

Just as we cannot be the salt of the earth, as Bishop Pace taught, by remaining as a singular "clump" in the cultural hall, we cannot build Zion by merely isolating ourselves in a bomb shelter or the basement storeroom surrounded by all of our freeze-dried food, guns, and ammo. No, the parable of the talents reminds us that we must be preparing for the Second Coming spiritually, not just temporally. Of course, there will be calamities and tribulations that will call upon all of our best temporal preparation. As members of the Church, we have been counseled repeatedly for decades by the prophetic leaders of the Lord's Church concerning the importance of being financially prepared and of having adequate food and fuel stored in case of need. These preparations are vital and must not be ignored. However, temporal preparedness will go only so far. Having world-class food storage does not mean we are adequately prepared to meet the Savior. No wonder the Church has counseled us to "avoid being caught up in extreme efforts to anticipate catastrophic events."[11] The primary message of this parable is that as we go about the Lord's work of *loving* and *serving,* we will be *becoming* ready to greet Him in His glory.

THE PARABLE OF THE SHEEP AND GOATS

Matthew 25:31–46

Many Palestinian shepherds in the Holy Land have both goats and sheep in their flocks. Sheep and goats are close relatives, biologically speaking, and each is a valuable resource to the shepherd and his family in an agricultural economy. Sheep provide wool—a valuable commodity that is spun into fabric, which then can be used in numerous ways. Goats provide milk—a valuable commodity used by the shepherd's family for food products. Although distinct from each other in various ways, both sheep and goats are useful, each in its own way. Jesus's parable of the sheep and goats is about *separation* more than *species.* It's not about the relative value of sheep versus goats, nor their respective habits or hygiene, though it is interesting to take note of them. Interpreting this parable, some scholars have characterized goats as overly independent. Thus, they must be driven by the shepherd, rather than following him as sheep generally do. That may be true. But that isn't really what the parable is all about. It is about a judgment day that accompanies the Second Coming—the separation of the righteous from the wicked "as a shepherd divideth his sheep from the goats" (Matthew 25:32).

When my family and I lived in Israel, we often saw Bedouin shepherds bringing their sheep and goats back to the camp each evening after grazing in the Judean hills. Although goats and sheep grazed together during the day, they were separated to their respective folds at night. It was easy to understand why Jesus used such familiar imagery in His teaching. Moreover, it was not unique to Him—others taught using similar symbolism. Old Testament prophets spoke of the coming Messiah as a shepherd (see Psalm 23, Isaiah 40, Ezekiel 34) and characterized God's faithful, covenant people as His sheep (see Psalm 95:7). Jesus built upon this symbolism when He declared Himself as the Good Shepherd and said that His sheep know His voice (see John 10:16). So it is quite understandable that He used that same imagery as He, in response to the disciples' questions, taught them concerning His glorious return and the day of judgment. Interestingly, the Master doesn't condemn goats. He merely uses the imagery of separation. The sheep—His sheep and lambs—are gathered to Him on his right hand, a scriptural symbol denoting approbation, acceptance, power, and heirship. They are the righteous who have watched for the Lord's return and have prepared themselves spiritually for that day. They are on the right hand of the Savior—"blessed of my Father" (Matthew 25:34).

Then shall the King say unto them on his right hand, Come, ye blessed of my Father, inherit the kingdom prepared for you from the foundation of the world:

For I was an hungred, and ye gave me meat: I was thirsty, and ye gave me drink: I was a stranger, and ye took me in:

Naked, and ye clothed me: I was sick, and ye visited me: I was in prison, and ye came unto me.

Then shall the righteous answer him, saying, Lord, when saw we thee an hungred, and fed thee? or thirsty, and gave thee drink?

When saw we thee a stranger, and took thee in? or naked, and clothed thee?

Or when saw we thee sick, or in prison, and came unto thee?

And the King shall answer and say unto them, Verily I say unto you, Inasmuch as ye have done it unto one of the least of these my brethren, ye have done it unto me.

—Matthew 25:34–40

There is a common phrase we often hear today—"He (She) is so-and-so's right-hand man (woman)." It implies a trusted, dependable, loyal associate who can be counted on at all times. In the scriptural sense, the notion of being on the Lord's right hand characterizes not only those who do good and honorable things in the world, but those who make and keep sacred covenants. King Benjamin taught his people that "because of the covenant which ye have made ye shall be called the children of Christ, his sons, and his daughters; for behold, this day he hath spiritually begotten you; . . . your hearts are changed through faith on his name" (Mosiah 5:7). He reminded them that as they take upon themselves by covenant the name of Christ and are obedient to God, they "shall be found at the right hand of God" (Mosiah 5:8–9). Likewise, Alma the Elder was taught by the Lord that those who hear the voice of the Master, who affirmatively respond to His invitation to take upon themselves gospel covenants, and who faithfully keep those covenants "shall have a place eternally at my right hand" (Mosiah 26:23–24).

As a "parable of preparation," the essential message is how the Savior's disciples—both ancient and modern—keep their covenants and how that is manifest in what they are *doing* and becoming as they wait for their Master's return. The sheep of the Good Shepherd—those on His right side, those who will be prepared to be caught up to meet the Messiah as He descends from heaven—are those who serve Him by loving and serving others.

Principle of Preparedness
LOVE, SERVE, AND MINISTER TO GOD'S CHILDREN

On the shore of the Sea of Galilee, the resurrected Christ reminded Peter (and the other disciples) that they demonstrate their love for the Savior by serving and loving others. "Feed my sheep," "Feed my lambs," "Feed my sheep," Jesus commanded (see John 21:15–17). The relationship of this teaching to the parable of the sheep and goats, uttered by Christ just days earlier on the Mount of Olives, is apparent. "Feeding" the sheep of the Good Shepherd's fold was the Apostles' responsibility as they waited upon Jesus's promised return. But it is not just the work of Apostles. It is what righteous disciples do—those on the right hand of the King of kings—as they patiently and faithfully prepare for the Second Coming, whether in the first century or in a century yet to come. For, as the Book of Mormon prophet-king Benjamin taught, "when ye are in the service of your fellow beings ye are only in the service of your God" (Mosiah 2:17).

> *Feed the flock of God which is among you, taking the oversight thereof not by constraint, but willingly; not for filthy lucre, but of a ready mind; neither as being lords over God's heritage, but being ensamples to the flock. And when the chief Shepherd shall appear, ye shall receive a crown of glory that fadeth not away.*
>
> —1 Peter 5:2–4

With the parable of the talents, Jesus taught His disciples to be anxiously engaged until He comes again. The works in which they should be anxiously engaged were clearly highlighted in the parable of the sheep and goats. The parable of the ten virgins, with its emphasis on continual preparedness, reminds disciples that they must be in it for the long haul, because the work is incessant and the wait may be longer than expected.

THE PARABLE OF THE TEN VIRGINS

Matthew 25:1–13

One of the most familiar of all of Jesus's parables, the parable of the ten virgins was the first parable given in direct response to the disciples' questions regarding when the Second Coming would occur. President Wilford Woodruff taught that this parable was directed exclusively to members of the Church—both wise and foolish virgins represented those who had already come into the kingdom by covenant.[12] The context for each of the parables of preparation seems to confirm that the intended audience was specifically the Apostles and generally all other disciples who had come unto Christ through ordinances and covenants of the gospel. As "witnesses of God at all times . . . and in all places" (Mosiah 18:9), theirs was a special obligation. They were not only to be prepared for the Savior's glorious return but also had a covenantal obligation to help others prepare for that day. To lift another, one must stand on higher ground. Thus, the main message of this parable is that of the need for true disciples to be righteous and ever ready for the Second Coming because, as Jesus taught, "ye know neither the day nor the hour wherein the Son of man cometh" (Matthew 25:13). Additionally, this parable addresses the *when* question, which sheds further light on the preparation, or lack thereof, by the virgins—members of the Church.

"Then shall the kingdom of heaven be likened unto ten

virgins, which took their lamps, and went forth to meet the bridegroom" (Matthew 25:1).

It was the custom (and still is in some traditional Middle-Eastern communities) that the groom and his kinfolk traveled by procession to the home of the bride. Waiting to greet them were the bride's family members and friends. (The virgins of the parable were young women who, like today's bridesmaids, were close friends of the bride and assisted her in her marriage preparations.) Leaving behind her parents, family, and all other associations, the bride would then go with her husband to live with his parents and family. As the two clans, or families, were joined by this marriage (often an arranged marriage in which the bride and groom had not met or were only casually acquainted with each other), the procession then returned to the home of the groom. (Thus the phrase "went forth to meet the bridegroom." The "waiting upon" the bridegroom occurred at both places.) This traditional marriage—the procession and celebration that accompanied the wedding—began in the evening and often went on for many hours or even days, in some cases. Thus the need for lamps to provide light for the nighttime procession and festivities. Some have suggested that the "lamps" were actually torches carried by those in the processional. The cloth wrapped around the end of the stick had been saturated in olive oil. Others indicate that those going to and from the bride's home (and those waiting with her) held the small, household oil lamps that were commonly used. So which is it? Probably both. Whether it was a large torch held high or a tiny lamp held in the palm of a young woman's hand is immaterial to the meaning of the parable. Both required fuel, typically olive oil, to provide adequate light for the duration of the marriage celebration.

"And five of them were wise, and five were foolish.

"They that were foolish took their lamps, and took no oil with them:

"But the wise took oil in their vessels with their lamps" (Matthew 25:2–4).

Those who were foolish took only their filled lamps. But the wise, in addition to their lamps, took "vessels"—pottery flasks—containing a reserve supply of olive oil. A small Herodian lamp would hold enough oil to keep a lamp lit for a couple of hours. A vessel of oil would provide enough supply for many additional hours. Perhaps the groom's family did not live far from the bride's family. Could this have been a reason why the foolish assumed that the wedding procession would not take long and that reserve vessels of oil would be unnecessary? They could not imagine any reason for the groom to delay his coming. Yet he did. An hour late. Then another and another. The evening became late night. Darkness enveloped them, and soon they were overcome with fatigue. "While the bridegroom tarried, they all slumbered and slept" (Matthew 25:5). In the parable, the bridegroom's coming didn't occur when most of the people expected it. He was taking much longer than expected, and certainly longer than half the virgins had prepared for.

"And at midnight there was a cry made, Behold, the bridegroom cometh; go ye out to meet him" (Matthew 25:6).

There would not have been clocks in that day, so Jesus's use of the word "midnight" didn't necessarily mean precisely

12:00 a.m. but rather signified extreme lateness—the very last hour. That imagery was to teach His disciples that His coming would indeed be in "an hour when ye think not" (Luke 12:40). It won't be when we expect it or want it. In fact, there will yet come tribulations and challenges that will test our faith and endurance. It may even cause many of the faithful to wonder, "Why hasn't He come yet? How much longer must we endure?" (see Luke 12:45; D&C 45:26). As a result, all disciples must, like the wise virgins, prepare for a long night of watching and waiting for Him. We must fight off spiritual fatigue and natural-man impatience and tendency to distraction.

"Then all those virgins arose, and trimmed their lamps.

"And the foolish said unto the wise, Give us of your oil; for our lamps are gone out.

"But the wise answered, saying, Not so; lest there be not enough for us and you: but go ye rather to them that sell, and buy for yourselves.

"And while they went to buy, the bridegroom came; and they that were ready went in with him to the marriage: and the door was shut" (Matthew 25:7–10).

Clearly, Jesus was teaching that the "oil of preparedness" can be "purchased" only over time with faith and diligence. Reserves of readiness are "stored" drop by drop, day after day— even when the days are long and the nights are dark—when we feel physically, emotionally, and spiritually worn down or worn out. It is in those very moments when our individual reserves come into play, just as they did for the ten virgins.

Principle of Preparedness
BE EVER READY WITH RESERVES
OF RIGHTEOUSNESS

What did the foolish virgins—those who were caught un-prepared for the coming of the bridegroom—miss because of their unpreparedness? It wasn't their wedding. Why should it matter? The answer is that they missed out on the incredible celebration—the "feast of fat things" (Isaiah 25:6), the exqui-site rejoicing with family and friends, the dancing and singing, a special moment in time when all are free from the typical burdens, cares, and concerns of life. Most of all, they will have missed out on having a place of at the table of the Lord in His presence.

What, then, is the "oil of preparedness" that must fill the lamps of the wise? How do we today fill our "vessels" so they will provide us with ready reserves at "midnight"—whatever hour of the day or night that comes? That will be the focus of the next chapter.

Chapter 5

WHAT WE MUST BECOME

Recently a colleague shared with me an experience he and several friends had with a Jewish rabbi. After making a presentation to the group, the rabbi entertained questions from the audience. Questions were asked about the Jewish concepts of Messiah—when the Messiah would come and what would happen when He does. The rabbi responded, "I don't worry too much about when the Messiah comes. I just live my life each day so as to be ready whenever Messiah comes among us. I try each day to do my little part at making the world a place where the Messiah would want to be." Although there is a wide array of Jewish beliefs regarding the coming of the Messiah—or even if there is a Messiah—this rabbi's view focused on the here and now rather than on some far-distant future messianic age. Despite years of studying and speculating about the coming of a Messiah, the rabbi had settled on a basic philosophy. He determined that how he lived his life, loved his family, and served his fellow men was the very essence of "watching and waiting" for that day.

There is a common declaration of belief that is often recited by Jews all over the world:

"I believe with a perfect faith in the coming of the Messiah, and though he tarry, I will wait daily for his coming."[13] The rabbi's actions seem to correlate perfectly with the idea of "waiting daily."

The perspective of the rabbi certainly reflects the intended message of Jesus's parable of the ten virgins. Perhaps we can learn from the Jews who have waited daily, with "perfect faith," for about four thousand years! If any people has ever had reason to long for or obsess over the coming of their Messiah, it is the Jews. As Latter-day Saints, we know that He has come, but still we await His return. We may be better served by learning how to wait patiently and faithfully, as many Jews have, than by spending an inordinate amount of time preoccupied with interpreting signs or "prepping" for the apocalypse, which could keep us from the kind of preparation we really need.

One woman told me that her patriarchal blessing informed her she would live to see many of the signs of the Second Coming, *but she wouldn't understand them!* That seems to be true for all of us to some degree. Why would the Lord give us signs we can be aware of but can't interpret? Perhaps because He doesn't want us to become overly anxious about details, deadlines, and all manner of speculation that may cause us to lose sight of or interest in simple truths.

The key to waiting patiently is to just keep living the gospel day by day. It's the "Sunday School answers"—praying always, reading the scriptures, repenting continually, striving to do a little better today than yesterday, living the Golden Rule, and loving the Lord. All of these help fill our oil lamps with what President Spencer W. Kimball called our "reservoirs of righteousness."[14] Not only do these drops of diligence prepare us for the Second Coming, they prepare us for times of trial—as well as for times of ease and prosperity, when it is easy to forget God and let our preparation lag. They will give us strength to wait longer than expected if necessary. Doing the best we can to keep all the commandments will bless us and prepare us! I could end this book right here with that thought, but I would like to bring more focus and emphasis to some areas specifically mentioned in the scriptures that also have important implications for our "righteous readiness" for the Second Coming. These passages don't list all the things we must *do* as much as they instruct us about *what* we must *become*, *where* we must *stand*, and *how* we must *love* in preparation for the Second Coming. They will give more meaning to the "Sunday School answers." I have divided them into separate chapters even though there will be some overlap. Let us now examine *what we must become.* The next chapters will discuss *where we must stand* and *how we should love* as we prepare for the Savior's glorious return and millennial reign on earth.

A TRUE AND UNSHAKABLE DISCIPLE OF CHRIST

Often when some shocking evil or tragedy or a new controversy that seems unprecedented happens in the world, we are shaken out of our daily grind and reminded of the signs of the times. Facebook and other social media become plastered with old quotes and prophecies by prophets and apostles of yesteryear predicting how all these things would happen and that we shouldn't really be surprised. We express disbelief and cluck our tongues and say how scary it is to live in these trying times. After one of these episodes, one or two of our former missionaries messaged Sister Top and me, saying, "We remember how you warned us about staying strong in the last days when you said, 'Everything that can be shaken will be shaken.'" We had paraphrased a sermon given by President Heber C. Kimball, who bluntly told priesthood leaders in 1857: "Go ahead, press forward, and we will gain the victory. We will overcome, because with those that do repent, if there are not more than three hundred men, we will whip out the unrighteous, for, says the Lord, *everything that can be shaken shall be, and that which cannot be shaken will remain.*"[15] Many of our missionaries remembered that and had stayed firm in the faith, steadfast and unshakable in their testimonies. Sadly, we noted at the same time that some of our beloved missionaries had already been pulled away during the ten years we had been home, some by issues and events we saw coming, others by things that were not even imagined at the time they served with us.

We all know someone who has been "shaken," and none of us need expect to go untested ourselves. There are now and will yet be tests we have not even supposed. Something that doesn't test us now may try us later. Some trials may be obvious, while others may be so subtle we don't realize that our faith and conviction are being eroded. Trials of faith that are difficult for some will be easy for others. We may pass great tests only to be tripped up by seemingly smaller, less significant issues. And thus, none of us can expect to be untouched by tests, trials, and tribulations as the prophesied signs unfold around us. Nonetheless, we can prepare to meet the Savior by reaching the point that, like the prophet Jacob when confronted by the anti-Christ, we "[cannot] be shaken" (Jacob 7:5).

GUIDED ALWAYS BY THE HOLY SPIRIT

The drop-by-drop, day-by-day filling of our "reservoirs of righteousness," as President Kimball emphasized, is done by all kinds of acts of faithfulness. But righteous readiness requires more than just *doing* deeds, however noble and good those deeds may be. There must be real *devotion to the Lord—becoming* true disciples, not just *doing* disciple things. Righteous readiness is manifest by how we live our lives outwardly every day, but even more by what we are becoming inwardly. "The Final Judgment is not just an evaluation of a sum total of good and evil acts—what we have *done*," Elder Dallin H. Oaks taught. "It is an acknowledgment of the final effect of our acts and thoughts—what we have *become*. It is not enough for anyone just to go through the motions. The commandments, ordinances, and covenants of the gospel are not a list of deposits required to be made in some heavenly account. The gospel of Jesus Christ is a plan that shows us how to become what our Heavenly Father desires us to become."[16]

For, to be quickened by Him and caught up with the saints to meet Him, we must be like Him. The "lamps" of the wise are not just for appearance or decoration to celebrate the coming Lord. The lamps within us must burn bright to illuminate the path and dissipate darkness, not only for ourselves but for others. That which sanctifies—makes holy—our good deeds and transforms those actions into lasting personal righteousness is the power of the Holy Ghost. Speaking of the parable of the ten virgins in our dispensation, the Lord has taught that "they that are wise and have received the truth, and have *taken the Holy Spirit for their guide,* and have not been deceived—verily I say unto you, they shall not be hewn down and cast into the fire,

> *In the parable [of the ten virgins], oil can be purchased at the market. In our lives, the oil of preparedness is accumulated drop by drop in righteous living. Attendance at sacrament meetings adds oil to our lamps, drop by drop over the years. Fasting, family prayer, home teaching, control of bodily appetites, preaching the gospel, studying the scriptures—each act of dedication and obedience is a drop added to our store. Deeds of kindness, payment of offerings and tithes, chaste thoughts and actions, marriage in the covenant for eternity—these, too, contribute importantly to the oil with which we can at midnight refuel our exhausted lamps.*
>
> —Spencer W. Kimball, *Faith Precedes the Miracle* (1972), 256

but shall abide the day" (D&C 45:57; emphasis added). Living daily in such a way as to have the companionship of the Holy Ghost is the best way to be assured that we are prepared for the Second Coming. Hearkening to—hearing and acting upon— the Spirit keeps our lamps continually full of the oil of spiritual preparation. As the world becomes filled with more subtle and beguiling evils—and as the sophisticated arguments to overlook such things increase—there will be even greater need for spiritual discernment. As King Benjamin warned his people, "I cannot tell you all the things whereby ye may commit sin; for there are divers ways and means, even so many that I cannot number them" (Mosiah 4:29). There are simply not commandments for every situation or circumstance. The First Presidency won't send out a new letter every week with a long list of exactly what the Saints must do to face the specific challenges of that week. Neither the Lord nor His servants work that way. In order to navigate the last days, we simply must have the Spirit with us, especially to give us peace, comfort, and confidence even when we don't have all the answers. If we don't have the companionship of the Holy Ghost, we can't be prepared for the companionship of Christ when He comes again.

For instance, Doctrine and Covenants, section 88, is fascinating for the spectacular signs of the Second Coming listed there (see verses 87–95). However, there are other less sensational, but far more glorious and important eternal truths in that section that teach us something essential about the Spirit we need with us on that great day (see verses 27–35). We learn there that we will be quickened or resurrected by a full portion of the Spirit we have already sought to receive in part in mortality. Those who have embraced celestial law will be quickened by a fulness of the Spirit and celestial glory. Those who have lived the terrestrial law will then be quickened by that spirit. Those who have lived a telestial law, or as a law unto themselves, will not be resurrected at all at His Coming but must wait until the end of the Millennium! It is the law of attraction on an eternal scale: we attract what we are; we reap what we sow. "For intelligence cleaveth unto intelligence; wisdom receiveth wisdom; truth embraceth truth; virtue loveth virtue; light cleaveth unto light; mercy hath compassion on mercy and claimeth her own; justice continueth its course and claimeth its own" (D&C 88:40).

> *Let our anxiety be centered upon this one thing, the sanctification of our own hearts, the purifying of our own affections, the preparing of ourselves for the approach of the events that are hastening upon us. . . . This should be our daily prayer. . . . Seek to have the Spirit of Christ, that we may wait patiently the time of the Lord, and prepare ourselves for the times that are coming. This is our duty.*
>
> —Brigham Young, *Deseret News,* May 1, 1861, 65

There are many things, as President Kimball enumerated, that contribute to our having the Spirit as our guide in these last days—more than can be adequately addressed in this book (or many books). However, there are a few things that seem to me to be particularly relevant today as we watch, wait, and prepare for the "great day of the Lord." They appear throughout the scriptures and in the teachings of the latter-day prophets and apostles. These things are not new or unique, but they are foundational, guiding, comforting, and protective.

FIRMLY GROUNDED IN THE WORD OF GOD

In the Joseph Smith Translation of Matthew 24, we read that as Jesus spoke of the signs that would precede His Second

Coming, He warned of "false Christs, and false prophets [who] shall show great signs and wonders, insomuch, that, if possible, they shall deceive the very elect, who are the elect according to the covenant" (JS—M 1:22). That is a frightening thought that can further exacerbate "Second Coming anxiety." No wonder some "men's hearts shall fail them" when they witness the growing commotion in all things (D&C 88:91) as we approach that day. A common adage in our vernacular certainly applies to these troubled times: "It's going to get worse before it gets better." The scriptural prophecies regarding the last days attest to that.

How can the Lord's disciples today "abide" that day without faltering and falling, even as they are assaulted by false prophets with their deceptive and destructive philosophies, as well as mockers and persecutors from the great and spacious building? How can we be, as the wise virgins, guided by the brilliant light of the Holy Spirit when darkness prevails? There is a safeguard: "And whoso treasureth up my word," the Lord promised, "shall not be deceived" (JS—M 1:37).

The scriptures indeed have power to insulate us against the "fiery darts of the adversary" (1 Nephi 15:24). Feasting upon the words of Christ—hearing and feeling His voice in the scriptures (see D&C 18:34–36)—adds to our "vessels" the oil of preparedness. President Ezra Taft Benson taught that the scriptures, particularly the Book of Mormon, empower us to face trials and tribulations and protect us from deception by those who would destroy.[17] No wonder President Thomas S. Monson exhorted the Saints to conscientiously and consistently immerse themselves in the study of the Book of Mormon: "My dear associates in the work of the Lord,

I implore each of us to prayerfully study and ponder the Book of Mormon each day. As we do so, we will be in a position to hear the voice of the Spirit, to resist temptation, to overcome doubt and fear, and to receive heaven's help in our lives."[18]

> *When I think of the Book of Mormon, I think of the word power. The truths of the Book of Mormon have the power to heal, comfort, restore, succor, strengthen, console, and cheer our souls. . . . I promise that as you prayerfully study the Book of Mormon every day, you will make better decisions—every day. I promise that as you ponder what you study, the windows of heaven will open, and you will receive answers to your own questions and direction for your own life.*
>
> —Russell M. Nelson, "The Book of Mormon— What Would Your Life Be Like without It?" *Ensign*, November 2017, 62–63; emphasis in original.

Many years ago when I was teaching seminary, the Church began producing videos that showed how the Book of Mormon applied to the youth. One of my family's favorites was called "The Power of the Word." In this video portrayal, a faithful young Latter-day Saint woman (whom we will call Laura because I can't remember the name) has a roommate who meets a very well-spoken and good-looking young man who is an atheist. The young man is very interested in Laura's roommate and wants to date her. As he does, he attempts to draw her away from her LDS faith with his "sophisticated" modern ideas about how God is an old-fashioned and naive concept. As Laura tries to answer his taunts about their religion and to save her friend, she becomes increasingly frustrated that she can't compete with his flattering words. In fact, the young man convinces her roommate that he loves her and invites her to go away with him to a cabin for a fun-filled weekend—and she accepts. Laura knows what that means. She prays and searches her scriptures fervently to find an answer to bring her roommate to her senses. While reading Jacob 7 and the story of Sherem the anti-Christ, she realizes what is really going on. When the scheming suitor arrives to pick up the roommate, Laura confronts him in front of her roommate, exposing the real reasons he is trying to wear down the faith of her friend. He, like Sherem, was "labor[ing] diligently that he might lead away the [heart]" (Jacob 7:3) of this naive young woman. If he could get her to doubt the reality of God and the need for His teachings, her resolve would waver and he could have another conquest. As Laura calls him out on this, her roommate does waver—about going with this young man. Disgustedly, he leaves without her, unable to persuade her that he had her best interests at heart.

In a similar and all-too-real way, my wife and I have been recently concerned with the number of members of the Church who succumb to the seemingly sophisticated and enlightened teachings of those who encourage doubt about doctrine or history. Many voices, inside and outside of the Church, have been proclaiming that there is nothing wrong with doubt because everyone has doubts. This part is true. Yet, they then say we should doubt everything! It is normal—in fact, healthy! Only ignorant people are nondoubting believers. Prove everything through reason. Some have called this the celebration or glori-fication of doubt. This is the untrue part. As we searched the scriptures to understand exactly what role doubt should play in our lives, we learned that doubt is like a hot potato taken right out of a very hot oven. If you hold onto it for too long, it will burn through your faith and testimony. We saw what happened to Peter when he began to doubt and fear as he walked upon the sea (see Matthew 14:24–33). We learned that doubt creates fear. We learned that doubt, when not dealt with in faith, weakens our resolve to keep the commandments, as Laura's room-mate found out. The Lord Himself clearly commands us *not* to doubt (see Mormon 9:27; D&C 6:36). We can choose faith over doubt and fear.[19] If we handle our questions and concerns with faith, not doubt, they can actually lead to greater testi-mony and more oil in our lamps of personal preparation.

We see a great example in the Joseph Smith story in the Pearl of Great Price of how Joseph handled his questions with faith (see Joseph Smith—History 1:5–17). We know what great manifestations and miracles came of that. "The power of the word" empowers us to stand up against "sophisticated" but deceptive teachings and cut through them with the sharpness of a two-edged sword (see D&C 6:2; 11:2; 12:2; 14:2; 33:1). As I counsel with missionaries, students, Church members, and family who struggle to hold onto their faith, I testify that the answer to doubt is and always will be faith. And the way to greater faith is always found in those time-tested "Sunday School answers": studying the scriptures and the words of liv-ing prophets, keeping the Spirit in our lives, praying sincerely, keeping covenants, worthily partaking of the sacrament, and worshiping the Lord on His holy day. Some don't want to hear those simple answers; they are looking beyond the mark for something more complex and sophisticated. If you are bored by the Sunday School answers, take heed!

Alma testified that the word of God had a more powerful effect upon the people than the sword, or anything else, for that matter. As he sought to reclaim his people who were dwindling in unbelief, he determined to "try the virtue of the word of God" (Alma 31:5). When in doubt, it is never a bad idea to search the scriptures! Knowing them and being intimately familiar with the doctrine taught therein and the spirit that emanates from them will fortify your faith and preparedness.

Let me give you another pertinent example. My wife had an experience many years ago with a would-be prophet who tried to teach her false doctrine and draw her into his circle of influence. One day a man called her about an article she had published, expressing great interest. He wanted her to know that he had some special insight into the subject. He called a few times to discuss it with her, giving her only bits and pieces of his so-called experiences, but not enough to trigger any serious concerns. Finally, he asked to meet with her at my office to share his message and see if she showed any interest. Being polite, she agreed. When he came to the Joseph Smith Building on the BYU campus, we met him on the first floor. Curiously, he had a woman, not his wife, with him. As we chatted on the way upstairs to my office, we learned that she believed in what he had to say and had recently quit her job at Church headquarters to help this man spread his message. That didn't seem like a good trade to us. (Could have been a lie!)

He proceeded to tell us of a special revelation he had received on the subject in question, all of which contradicted specific teachings in the scriptures. Our "scripture antennae" went up! We pointed out several relevant passages. Dismissing those scriptures, he told us that he had met with one of the Apostles and was told that he was commissioned to share his teachings secretly. Immediately, more scriptures came to our minds. Early in the history of the Church, the Saints were taught that there could be no secret teachings. Only those leaders publicly accepted by common consent could preach to the Church (see D&C 42:11–12). Further, only the prophet could receive revelation for the Church (see D&C 43:1–7). Thus, it was easy for Wendy to reject this man's claim that he had received some special commission to deliver secret teachings or practices to members of the Church.

When we wouldn't accept the man's "revelations," he became contentious. The female companion said nothing the whole time. Wendy wanted to say out loud, and probably should have, "You need to get away from this man. He is teaching you false doctrine and leading you astray!" Instead, we kindly invited the man to leave and take his friend with him. At first, he refused. But when I threatened to call campus police, they finally left in a huff. The incident was upsetting to both Wendy and me. We were so very grateful at that moment for the holy scriptures that can keep us safely anchored in the gospel.

Though my wife and I have a fairly extensive background in scriptures because we teach and write about them, I believe you don't necessarily have to know exact scripture references to know when someone is teaching false doctrine. If you make a continual, sincere effort to study and apply the scriptures in your life and family, the Spirit will make you feel uncomfortable when false doctrine is taught. We find that almost all faithful members of the Church have this spiritual intuition. It is not available only to a select few, but can be cultivated by every member. Even children can have it. What we must become is *firmly grounded in the scriptures.* We are also blessed to have prophets, seers, and revelators, whose right it is to interpret scriptures; they can help us to better understand them and to apply their teachings to our own lives.

LOYALTY TO THE LORD'S ANOINTED

Hearkening to the words of prophets also fills our lamps of preparation drop by drop. Possessing the keys of the kingdom and sustained as prophets, seers, and revelators, they give us protective instructions, exhortations, and promises "when moved upon by the Holy Ghost" that "shall be the will of the Lord, shall be the mind of the Lord, shall be the *word of the Lord,* shall be the voice of the Lord, and the power of God unto salvation" (D&C 68:4; emphasis added). Interestingly, in this same revelation the Lord speaks of His servants as those to whom "it shall be given to know the signs of the times, and the signs of the coming of the Son of Man" (D&C 68:11). We can look to the Lord's anointed to help us recognize the signs of the times, understand their meaning, and prepare for the Second Coming. As the day of the Lord's coming draws nearer, "iniquity shall abound, the love of men shall wax cold" (JS—M 1:30), and our need to walk in the path illuminated by prophets of God will dramatically increase.

There are many inspiring stories from Church history re-counting how our pioneer forebears were blessed and protected by following the counsel and direction of living prophets. One of my favorites not only demonstrates willingness to obey a difficult call from a prophet but is also a metaphor that, in my estimation, has particular relevance for us today. It recounts the incredible faith and determination of Arabelle Smith and her husband, Stanford. They were among the early pioneers called to colonize southern Utah and northern Arizona. The Smiths were in the company that had to blaze a trail through one of the most dangerous canyons in the intermountain area, which was known as Hole-in-the-Rock. Today, the remnants of Hole-in-the-Rock descend into Lake Powell, located on the border of Utah and Arizona, and it doesn't seem so ominous. In the nineteenth century, however, the treacherous descent down "the Hole" to the Colorado River required many men to hang onto ropes tied to the back of each wagon to help it slowly de-scend the canyon. Some would also tie cut cedar trees or their balky mules to their wagons as an additional braking system. The Smith family's account of their perilous journey through "the Hole" not only is a witness of their faith and determina-tion but can also serve as a parable, so to speak, for us and our needs today. In a symbolic way, this true story teaches us that our safety in these last days leading up to the Second Coming depends in large measure upon our "hanging on" to the words of living prophets.

The main body of Hole-in-the-Rock pioneers successfully made their way through the treacherous canyon and crossed the Colorado River on January 26, 1880. What should have been a time of great relief and jubilation was actually a time of sheer panic for the Smiths. Through a series of unfortunate circumstances, the wagon containing all their earthly belongings as well as their three little children was inadvertently left behind. Stanford had spent the day helping others down the "Hole" and onto rafts across the river. Belle, with babe in arms and the other children asleep in the wagon, watched from the top of the canyon. After all of the wagons—or so they thought—had successfully navigated the most dangerous part of their trip, "Stanford looked around for his family and wagon, but they were nowhere in sight. He dropped his shovel and climbed to the top of the crevice.

"There, huddled, in a heap of tattered quilts on packed dirty snow he found his wife, her baby swathed in blankets in her arms.

"'Stanford, I thought you'd never come,' she exclaimed.

"'But where are the other children, and the wagon?' he asked.

"'They're over there. They moved the wagon back while they took the others down.' She pointed to the rusty stovepipe showing above a huge sandstone boulder.

"'With me down there helping get their wagons on the raft, I thought someone would bring my wagon down.'"[20]

Stanford and Belle were left with no options but to try to get their wagon down on their own. After tying logs and a mule to the back of the wagon to serve as a braking system, Stanford realized that there was no one who could hold onto the rope to provide additional help to avoid a runaway wagon.

"I'll do the holding back," Belle resolutely declared.

Left with no other options—having Belle drive the wagon would be too dangerous for her—Stanford agreed. "Hold as tight as you can," he said. After placing their three children in a safe spot away from the canyon and promising them that they would return, Belle and Stanford began the dangerous descent.

"Stanford took her arm and they walked to the top of the crevice, where hand in hand they looked down—10 feet of loose sand, then a rocky pitch as steep as the roof of a house and barely as wide as the wagon—below that a dizzy chute down the landing place, once fairly level but now ploughed up with wheels and boots. Below that, they could not see, but Stanford knew what was down there—boulders, washouts, dugways, like narrow shelves. But it was the first drop of 150 feet that frightened him.

"'I am afraid we can't make it,' he exclaimed.

"'But we've got to make it,' she answered calmly.

"They went back to the wagon where Stanford checked the harness, the axles, the tires, the brakes. He looked at Belle, and felt a surge of admiration for this brave beautiful girl. They had been called to go to San Juan, and they would go. With such a wife, no man could retreat."[21]

Remarkably, Stanford Smith was able to get his wagon down the canyon. More remarkably—even miraculously—Belle Smith made it down as well. Covered in dust from head to toe, battered and bruised and dragged much of the way, there she was—holding onto the rope. She wouldn't let go. She held as tight to that rope of safety as Lehi urges us to hold to the iron rod.

Make no mistake about it, brothers and sisters; in the months and years ahead, events will require of each member that he or she decide whether or not he or she will follow the First Presidency. Members will find it more difficult to halt longer between two opinions (see 1 Kings 18:21).

. . . This is a hard doctrine, but it is a particularly vital doctrine in a society which is becoming more wicked. In short, brothers and sisters, not being ashamed of the gospel of Jesus Christ includes not being ashamed of the prophets of Jesus Christ.

—Neal A. Maxwell, "Meeting the Challenges of Today," BYU Devotional, October 10, 1978

Prophets of God have reminded us that there are yet "tight places" that we—both the Church institutionally and its members individually—must go through as we prepare for the Second Coming. "Holding fast"—hearing and hearkening—to prophetic counsel is as vital to our safety today as it was in ancient days. Though the dangers and threats may be much different, we may also feel battered and bruised before we are through!

During a particular time of turmoil in the world, as Saints wondered anew if the Lord's Second Coming was imminent, President Harold B. Lee stated: "Your safety and ours depends upon whether or not we follow the ones whom the Lord has placed to preside over his church." He explained, "There will be some things that take patience and faith. You may not like what comes from the authority of the Church. It may contradict your political views. It may contradict your social views. It may interfere with some of your social life. But if you listen to these things, as if from the mouth of the Lord himself, with patience and faith, the promise is that the 'gates of hell shall not prevail against you: yea, and the Lord God will disperse the powers of darkness before you, and cause the heavens to shake for your good, and his name's glory.' (D&C 21:6.)"[22]

Filling our oil lamps of preparedness and living in "righteous readiness" requires that we hold on for dear life, giving heed to the warning voices of the watchmen and the protective, comforting counsel of the Lord's anointed. What we must become is *loyal followers and defenders of the prophets.* We can be like President Lorenzo Snow, who made it a rule "to honor and reverence the Priesthood" even when he saw things in the leaders that did not harmonize with his own views. If Church leaders didn't always act or speak as he thought they should, Lorenzo threw a "mantle of charity over improper things." Exemplifying loyalty to and a recognition of the role of the prophets of the Lord and other ordained leaders, he declared, "I feel like David of old, who would not raise his hand against the anointed of God even though Saul had sought to take his life." He concluded, "We have got to submit to things that do not agree with our ideas if we remain true to God."[23]

CONVERTED UNTO THE LORD

President Wilford Woodruff taught that the virgins in Jesus's parable represented the members of the Church:

"I expect that the Saviour was about right when he said, in reference to the members of the church, that five of them were wise and five were foolish; for when the Lord of heaven comes in power and great glory to reward every man according to the deeds done in the body, if he finds one-half of those professing to be members of his church prepared for salvation, it will be as many as can be expected judging by the course that many are pursuing."[24]

While there is some question as to the context and ultimate aim of President Woodruff's comments, I am still left to wonder, why did he think that only one-half of Church members of his day would be "prepared for salvation" when the Savior comes again? What was the "course that many [were] pursuing" (or not pursuing)? What is the fundamental difference in spiritual preparedness between the wise and foolish? Although there are certainly many answers to that question, President Spencer W. Kimball said that it really boils down to devotion. The unwise virgins, he declared, were not "necessarily corrupt and reprobate, but they were knowing people who were foolishly unprepared for the vital happenings that were to affect their eternal lives. They had the saving, exalting gospel, *but it had not been made the center of their lives.* They knew the way but *gave only a small measure of loyalty and devotion.*"[25]

The sixteenth chapter of Helaman in the Book of Mormon is a pattern and a warning for our day. As the birth of Christ drew nearer, even after the warnings of Samuel, the Lamanite prophet, wickedness and corruption spread throughout the land of both the Nephites and the Lamanites. Unlike in our day, they had been given a time frame, five years, for the first coming of Christ. Most gave no heed to Samuel's words. Many of those who initially did listen lost their faith before the end of the five-year time period they were warned about. Even as "great signs" and "wonders" were given to the people, and the words of the prophets and the scriptures began to be fulfilled, and angels appeared unto wise men and "did declare unto them glad tidings of great joy" (Helaman 16:13–14), most of the people fell away. Just having access to the scriptures and the prophets was not enough. They did not internalize them or maintain testimonies of them. Instead, they stopped treasuring them and began to rationalize them away with arguments based on mortal reasoning that is still used today (see Helaman 16:16–22). As a result, *all save it were the most believing part of them,* both of the Nephites and also of the Lamanites, . . . began to depend upon their own strength and upon their own wisdom" (Helaman 16:15; emphasis added). Notice that knowing the signs and even the time of the Lord's coming made no difference except for "the most believing part of them." This is a very sobering phrase indeed.

Every member of the Church has taken upon himself or herself sacred covenants. Every member of the Church has been confirmed and received the gift of the Holy Ghost. Unfortunately, not every member of the Church has lived worthily and sought faithfully to actually have the constant companionship of the Holy Ghost and, like the wise virgins, taken Him as a guide. Not all members have testimonies of the restored gospel, even though they could. Some have received that spiritual witness through the power of the Holy Ghost, but then let that spiritual light in their lives dim or flicker out. Even with a testimony—even after having had personal, spiritual experiences—one may not be totally converted and consecrated. "A testimony is spiritual knowledge of truth obtained by the power of the Holy Ghost," Elder David A. Bednar said. "Continuing conversion is *constant* devotion to the revealed truth we have received—with a heart that is willing and for righteous reasons. Knowing that the gospel is true is the essence of testimony. *Consistently being true to the gospel is the essence of conversion.* We should know the gospel is true and be true to the gospel."[26] Elder Bednar insightfully observed that the foolish virgins in the parable had the "lamp of testimony" but lacked the "oil of conversion." This seems to be the fundamental difference, the key to possessing "reservoirs of righteousness." As Elder Bednar observed, the kind of conversion and consecration that makes us worthy to be caught up with the Savior when He comes in glory is acquired consistently, daily, drop by drop in faith and devotion that draw us near to the Holy Spirit. We will know when we have the Spirit with us because we will experience the fruit of the Spirit: "love, joy, peace, longsuffering, gentleness, goodness, faith, meekness, temperance: against such there is no law" (Galatians 5:22–23). We will know that we have the Spirit because the fire and light of testimony will not only be continually burning within us but will grow brighter and stronger over the years. We will be filled with a desire to give all we have and are. Nothing will be more important to us than the Lord. The scriptures and the prophets will become dearer and dearer to us as we work tirelessly to prepare our earthly portion of the kingdom that will greet our Savior when He comes back to rule and reign on earth. If we are truly converted, we will never feel that we cannot fall.

Several years ago, in a CES devotional for young single adults, Elder Jeffrey R. Holland told the story of an LDS basketball player who had transferred from a Utah school to play basketball for a different school out of state. He came to town with his new school to play in a game against his former Utah school. What transpired both at the game and in the days afterward left Elder Holland "furious." He explained:

"What happened in that game has bothered me to this day, and I am seizing this unusual moment to get it off my chest. The vitriolic abuse that poured out of the stands on this young man's head that night—a Latter-day Saint, returned missionary, newlywed who paid his tithing, served in the elders' quorum, gave charitable service to the youth in his community . . . what was said and done and showered upon him that night, and on his wife and their families, should not have been experienced by any human being anywhere anytime, whatever his sport, whatever his university or whatever his personal decisions had been about either of them."

Elder Holland further explained that when all this was happening, the legendary coach of the visiting team said to the young man, "What is going on here? You are the hometown boy who has made good. These are your people." Then this damning question: "Aren't most of these people members of your Church?"

What transpired at the game became the focus of comments in sports talk shows and was posted on message boards in the days that followed the game. One person wrote: "Listen. We are talking basketball here, not Sunday School. If you can't stand the heat, get out of the kitchen. We pay good money to see these games. We can act the way we want. We check our religion at the door."

Listen to how Elder Holland responded to that sentiment:

"'We check our religion at the door'? Lesson number one for the establishment of Zion . . . : You never 'check your religion at the door.' Not ever. . . .

"That kind of discipleship cannot be—it is not discipleship at all. . . .We are 'to stand as witnesses of God at all times and in all things, and in all places that ye may be in,' *not* just some of the time, in a few places, or when our team has a big lead."[27]

If we want to be with Christ or to be caught up to meet Him when He comes, we must become His true and unshakable disciples. As such we can *never* "check our religion at the door," at any door. Not the door to sports, not the door to politics, not to public opinion, not to family relationships, not to our private lives or opinions, not to our business dealings, our profession, or academics, not the door to the place where we are hated, persecuted, humiliated, offended, abused, or harmed, or even the door to where we are sure that we are right. You get the idea. Nothing excuses us from seeking and retaining the Spirit in our lives, applying the scriptures, and following the prophets. True and unshakable disciples of Christ are determined to imitate Christ under all conditions and repent continually to reach that goal, laying their all on the altar. Becoming such a disciple opens a most important door: the door to the marriage feast of the Lamb of God when He returns to claim His own (see Revelation 19:6–9).

Chapter 6

"STAND YE IN HOLY PLACES"

In addition to *what we must become* as we prepare to meet the Savior at His Second Coming, modern scripture reveals that there are important places *where we must stand*—places we must be associated with and to which we must be gathered when Christ returns. These places are sacred sanctuaries meant to prepare, protect, and perfect us. In three specific passages in the Doctrine and Covenants, the Saints are commanded to "stand in holy places" (45:32; 101:22) and "be not moved" (87:8). In each case, that charge is given in the context of signs of the last days and the required spiritual preparation for the Second Coming. What does the Lord mean by this?

Clearly, the term *stand,* as used in these passages, means more than just being passively present. It implies being *firmly grounded, rooted, or affixed.* When coupled with the phrase *be not moved,* it obtains an even greater meaning of being *immovable, steadfast, unwavering, unshakable.* While the scriptural phrase "stand in holy places" is not always connected to a specific location or place, it always involves a state of holiness, a condition of righteousness, obedience, or purity. Within the context of both an actual geographical place and a spiritual condition, we see that there are places—"holy places"—where if disciples will *stand,* in the truest sense of that word, holiness is obtained and the oil of spiritual preparation can flow into our lives. Let me suggest four such holy places. If we are found steadfastly standing in, building up, being built by, and defending these holy places, we will come to find Christ there even before He returns. Standing in holy places helps us become familiar and comfortable with Him so we can be ready to receive Him at His glorious return. As the world descends into prophesied commotion, and as wickedness and fear abound, these holy places will provide support, strength, and protection.

THE HOME AND FAMILY

"While salvation is an individual matter, exaltation is a family matter," President Russell M. Nelson has taught. He further explained, "When a family is sealed in the temple, that family may become as eternal as the kingdom of God itself."[28] The family is the very pattern of heaven. Because of this, the family is a holy institution and the home is a holy place, as sacred as any other. As such, it also becomes ground zero for Satan's attacks in the last days. We must stand with and for families, battling until that very last day to preserve and protect the divinely ordained family. And we must help each member of our own families come to know the Savior and be prepared to worthily greet Him when He comes again. The "weapons" to be used in this important battle are, as outlined in "The Family:

A Proclamation to the World": "faith, prayer, repentance, forgiveness, respect, love, compassion, work, and wholesome recreational activities."[29] Spiritual preparation for the Second Coming is not just an individual enterprise. It, too, is a "family affair."

> *The most important of the Lord's work you will ever do will be within the walls of your own home.*
>
> —Harold B. Lee, *Teachings of Presidents of the Church: Harold B. Lee* (2000), 134

In Satan's war on individuals, families, and family values, his arrows (or in today's world we could say bullets, bombs, and missiles) of destruction are flying all around us, our children, and our grandchildren. Unfortunately, many of those satanic weapons of war are not easy to see until we or one of our loved ones becomes seriously wounded. Because Satan's warfare can be so stealthy, I have often wished there were some form of Star Wars–like "force field" over my house that could intercept and destroy all evil influences threatening my family. Wouldn't it be nice if we could buy cans of protective coating we could spray on our children, or spiritual Kevlar clothing that would repel any and all "fiery darts of the adversary" (1 Nephi 15:24)? But it doesn't work that way. There is, however, something that does work. The Apostle Paul spoke of a protective spiritual endowment called the "armour of God" that enables us to "stand against the wiles of the devil" (Ephesians 6:11). This armor and its companion "shield of faith" cannot be applied merely from the *outside*. They must be developed from the *inside*. Their development is not a one-time event but rather an ongoing process that requires determination, hard work, and patience. That is where our homes become "holy places" vital in our last-days spiritual preparation. "The home and family have vital roles in cultivating and developing personal faith and testimony," Elder M. Russell Ballard taught. "The family is the basic unit of society; the best place for individuals to build faith and strong testimonies is in *righteous homes filled with love*."[30]

> *Lest parents and children be "tossed to and fro," and misled by "cunning craftiness" of men who "lie in wait to deceive," our Father's plan requires that, like the generation of life itself, the shield of faith is to be made and fitted in the family.*
>
> —Boyd K. Packer, *Mine Errand from the Lord* (2008), 273

Several years ago, I was involved in a major study with my BYU colleague Dr. Bruce A. Chadwick that examined the role of religion in the lives of LDS youth and how religion helped influence teen behavior. Additionally, we looked at what parents were doing (or not doing) in their homes to help their children to become responsible and caring and to develop their own testimonies and personal spirituality. The results of these studies have been published in several books and articles.[31]

Through the years I have jokingly referred to the results of our studies of thousands of LDS youth and parents as "duh research" because the answers to our research questions were so obvious. We didn't find anything particularly new, novel, or Nobel Prize–worthy. Those factors we found most significant are the same things that prophets and apostles have for decades counseled parents to do in their homes and with their families. Seeking to obey gospel teaching and to heed prophetic counsel has powerful, positive effects on families and individuals. Duh! They may be like other "Sunday School answers," but family prayer, family home evening, scripture study, and gospel discussions in the home proved to be important building blocks in the development of faith in the Lord, commitment to covenants, and devotion to the Church and its teachings, *just as prophets had promised.*

Not surprisingly, we found that family religious practices such as family prayer, scripture study, and family home evening, as important as they are, did not, in and of themselves, create a faithful family or a home that is a "holy place." Those activities and behaviors are means to an end, not the end themselves, just like having specific Sunday rules and activities does not make a Sabbath day holy. Such practices create an environment where the Spirit resides and where hearts and souls are more fully turned to the Lord. Neither parents nor Church teachers and leaders can ceremoniously bestow testimonies on others. But we can facilitate those experiences and foster those influences that will provide a fertile seedbed for faith to grow.

Every time I am on an airplane, I am impressed with the instruction that in case of a loss of cabin pressure, oxygen masks will deploy. Adults traveling with children are instructed to place the masks over their own mouths and noses and *then* place them over the children's. I have thought about that instruction from a spiritual standpoint. The difficult and trying days of the end times are the emergency. Faith and testimony are the spiritual oxygen needed for survival. As parents, we stand in holy places when we seek to ensure that our homes are rich in that kind of spiritual oxygen that we and our children can breathe deeply. It is vital to our preparation for the Savior's return. "We live in a time of great trouble and wickedness," President Thomas S. Monson declared. "What will protect us from the sin and evil so prevalent in the world today? I maintain that a strong testimony of our Savior, Jesus Christ, and of His gospel will help see us through to safety."[32]

Holy places—houses of God—are filled with love, for "God is love" (1 John 4:8). If our homes are to be holy places, we must love God and our family members with perfect love. As we experience the Lord's infinite love for us, we are drawn to Him. The deeper we feel that love, the deeper we love Him and seek to follow Him and prepare ourselves to meet Him. Likewise, our righteous influence in the lives of our family members is diminished if they do not feel our perfect love and acceptance through sincere expressions of love and actions that clearly demonstrate it.

In my calling as a stake president, I have counseled with people who tell me they have never felt God's love in their lives. As I probe deeper, it becomes clear to me that, although there are often many reasons for this, the most common is that they don't feel loved and accepted by their parents. What a tragedy! Almost certainly the parents would say that they indeed love and accept their children. The disconnect seems to be in how that love is manifest. Just as our love for the Lord, shown in how we live His gospel, cannot be inconspicuous or subtle, neither can our love for our children and other family members. We need to live in such a way as to leave no doubt in their minds about our love for them.

Sometimes the spirit of familial love and acceptance and the holiness of our homes are tested by the actions and decisions of family members. Loving and accepting family members does not mean that we have to approve of their bad choices and sinful actions. The Lord's standards of righteousness need not—in fact must not—be compromised as we seek to make our homes holy places where each family member is preparing to meet the Savior. God's infinite and perfect love for all His children, whether they are on the path or not, should be the standard we seek in our homes and with our families.

More than once I have had members of my stake express despair over wayward or unbelieving children in terms such as this: "The Second Coming is so close, but my children will not be ready!" I remind them that we cannot force our loved ones to fill their oil lamps. We can only provide the oil—and that oil is our own commitment to and example of loving the Lord with all our hearts, our determination to live His gospel, our unquestioned love for our children, and our prayers and noble efforts in their behalf. Those elements constitute a "holy place" where we must firmly and unwaveringly stand and be not moved.

THE CHURCH

Amidst the Missouri persecutions, the Prophet Joseph Smith received a revelation in April 1838 at Far West that identified the official name of the Church as we have it today.

In that revelation, the Lord spoke of the Church and its stakes as gathering places that would be "for a defense, and for a refuge from the storm, and from wrath when it shall be poured out without mixture upon the whole earth" (D&C 115:6). In 1831, the Prophet, in an inspired prayer canonized as section 65 of the Doctrine and Covenants, declared: "Prepare ye the way of the Lord, prepare ye the supper of the Lamb, make ready for the Bridegroom" (D&C 65:3). In that prayer, it is stated that the Church, the kingdom of God "which is set up on the earth," is to prepare the world "for the days to come, in the which the Son of Man shall come down in heaven, clothed in the brightness of his glory" (D&C 65:5). Thus, the Church becomes a "holy place," a protective place, for those who are willing to put down their roots deep into the soil of the gospel found within the Church community.

Several years ago, when I was serving as president of the Illinois Peoria Mission, I had an experience that graphically taught how the Church is a "refuge from the storm." During a stake conference, just as the presiding General Authority began his instruction, the stake president received an urgent message informing him that a tornado was headed dangerously close to the Church building. The presiding authority, choosing wisdom as the better part of valor, dismissed the congregation from the chapel and cultural hall to the inside hallways, where the strength of the roof and walls would provide the most protection. It was a unique experience for all present, needless to say—perhaps the most memorable stake conference I have attended. After a short while, the "all's clear" alarm was sounded and we went back into the chapel to continue the conference.

When we left the Church building after the conference ended, we noticed that there had been considerable danger and damage in the surrounding neighborhoods. But for the several hundred Saints in the Church building that day, there was protection and peace, knowing we were standing in a "holy place."

I recognize that sometimes dedicated Church buildings are indeed damaged or even destroyed by natural disasters. Temples have been flooded; chapels have been struck by lightning or destroyed by fire. I am not saying that Church buildings, as dedicated holy places of the Lord, will never suffer physical damage. What I am saying is that those physical edifices are tangible reminders of very real spiritual promises the Lord has given His Saints.

That is the "moral of the story" to me. That day, in that place and at that time, the physical integrity of the Church building was strong enough to protect against the powerful storm outside. It was a powerful reminder to us that the spiritual strength of the Church—its doctrines, ordinances, programs, support ministry, service opportunities, and faithful fellowship with caring brothers and sisters in the gospel—provides protection against the wrath that is "poured out without mixture upon the whole earth" (D&C 115:6). Likewise, the Church, with all its God-given powers, prepares us for the Second Coming of Jesus Christ.

As all loving and caring parents would do for their children, our Father in Heaven has provided His children with all that is needed for them to be successful. He has given us the structure, guidance, opportunity, and everything else we need to return to His presence. Yet, virtually all of it requires that we choose membership and faithfulness in the Church of Jesus Christ and that we "be not moved." In addition, the Church has the capacities to provide resources, strength, support, and safety in numbers that are not available to individual families or members. If the Church didn't exist, we would naturally band together to create something like it. It may not be perfect, but it is by far the best organization on earth for the divinely ordained family both in time and in eternity. Cling to it steadfastly, attend regularly, participate fully, and drink deeply.

> *It is true that we attend our weekly Church meetings to participate in ordinances, learn doctrine, and be inspired, but another very important reason for attending is that, as a ward family and as disciples of the Savior Jesus Christ, we watch out for one another, encourage one another, and find ways to serve and strengthen each other. We are not just receivers and takers of what is offered at church; we are needed to be givers and suppliers.*
>
> —Bonnie L. Oscarson, "The Needs before Us," *Ensign*, November 2017, 26

A substantial number of members of the Church are individuals, perhaps the only members of the Church in their families. Thankfully, the Church is also a "defense" and a "refuge" for individuals who may not enjoy the added blessing of a faithful and spiritually supportive family. My wife, Wendy, is an example of how the Church blesses individuals as well as families. She had wonderful parents, whom she loved and who took good care of her and raised her as well as they knew how. Her father was not a member of the Church, and her mother, although a baptized member, was never really active in the Church. Wendy longed for something they couldn't give her at home. She writes, "The Church became my gospel family—seminary my father, Relief Society my mother, Church programs were like loving siblings who surrounded me with wholesome activities as I grew up. Members showed me by example how to apply gospel principles in my own life. Priesthood leaders who blessed me and administered ordinances to me were sources of stability and strength. Church was a spiritual safe place that nurtured me in the gospel. Seeing those families prepared me to have an eternal family of my own." Even if you don't think you need the Church, the people in the Church need you—your talents, your love, your support and encouragement!

As I mentioned, in my calling as stake president I periodically hear from people with family members who are falling away from the Church not because of sinfulness (as far as they know) but because of some perceived imperfection in the Church, its doctrine, policies, or leaders. Those leaving insist they can still be followers of Christ and good human beings. Certainly they can, to some degree. Yet, as harsh as it may sound, to ultimately reject the Church is to reject the chief cornerstone of that Church. He organized a church to bear His name, administer His ordinances, and feed His sheep when He was on the earth. Eternal life with all its promises and potential, including forever families, is made possible only through the Church. "And he gave some, apostles; and some, prophets; and some, evangelists; and some, pastors and teachers; for the perfecting of the saints, for the work of the ministry, for the edifying of the body of Christ: till we all come in the unity of the faith, and of the knowledge of the Son of God, unto a perfect man, unto the measure of the stature of the fulness of Christ" (Ephesians 4:11–13).

> *God's plan is in place. He is at the helm, and His great and powerful ship flows toward salvation and exaltation. Remember that we cannot get there by jumping out of the boat and trying to swim there by ourselves.*
>
> *Exaltation is the goal of this mortal journey, and no one gets there without the means of the gospel of Jesus Christ: His Atonement, the ordinances, and the guiding doctrine and principles that are found in the Church.*
>
> *It is the Church wherein we learn the works of God and accept the grace of the Lord Jesus Christ that saves us. It is within the Church that we form the commitments and covenants of eternal families that become our passport to exaltation. It is the Church that is powered by the priesthood to propel us through the unpredictable waters of mortality.*
>
> —M. Russell Ballard, "God Is at the Helm,"
> *Ensign,* November 2015, 26–27

Surely, we have seen some people leave with every intention to retain their faith in Christ and maintain strong values in life, but without the structure, ordinances, obligations, and blessings of the Church. Although it may start out well (at least in their minds and by outward appearance), we usually see them sliding into spiritual slothfulness, then doubt and confusion over what to believe after all, and finally atheism. Their families then face challenges they might not have faced if they had remained faithful, or they give up the tools that would have made those trials smoother, not to mention the infinite blessings they forfeit in this life and potentially in the next.

The Master further endorsed His Church when teaching His disciples where to find safety at His Second Coming. "And now I show unto you a parable. Behold, wheresoever the carcass is, there will the eagles be gathered together; so likewise shall mine elect be gathered from the four quarters of the earth" (JS—M 1:27). Where the Church is, safety and salvation will be found. There we will find the nourishment and strength we need to keep our lamps filled. Standing on the fringes, questioning every new policy or procedure change, and finding fault with Church leaders puts us at risk. Straddling the border, with one foot in the kingdom and one in the world, not wanting to be "too committed" to either, is not "standing in holy places." In a classic speech given at Brigham Young University many years ago that is just as relevant today, Elder Bruce R. McConkie warned, "Please do not put too much stock in some of the current views and vagaries that are afloat, but rather, turn to the revealed word, get a sound understanding of the doctrines, and *keep yourselves in the mainstream of the Church.*"[33]

I am a big fan of documentaries about wildlife. It is fascinating and instructive to observe how predators in nature attack their prey. Almost always the predator seeks out prey that is on the fringes of the herd or is sickly and weak. The herd becomes a protection against the predator and a support to the young and vulnerable. I see the same phenomenon generally in spiritual matters. Satan preys not only upon those who are spiritually weak and sickly, but also upon those on the fringes who are separating themselves from the herd and testing the limits of safety. Like the herd in nature, the Church is a protection for those who are young or weak in faith. The Church is a protection for the strong and the more mature as well. However, all of us at times are weak and vulnerable. That is the very reason why the Church is a "holy place" in which we can stand as we face the difficulties of the last day. There we can and do receive support and strength from fellow Church members whose faith we can rely on and who may have just the right words of encouragement and uplift we need at that moment. Thus, we need each other. We need the Church.

"In the Church we not only learn divine doctrine; we also experience its application," explained Elder D. Todd Christofferson. "As the body of Christ, the members of the Church minister to one another in the reality of day-to-day life. All of us are imperfect; we may offend and be offended. We often test one another with our personal idiosyncrasies. In the body of Christ, we have to go beyond concepts and exalted words and have a real 'hands-on' experience as we learn to 'live together in love.'

"This religion is not concerned only with self; rather, we are all called to serve. We are the eyes, hands, head, feet, and other members of the body of Christ, and even 'those members . . . which seem to be more feeble, are necessary.' We need these callings, and we need to serve. . . .

"If one believes that all roads lead to heaven or that there are no particular requirements for salvation, he or she will see no need for proclaiming the gospel or for ordinances and covenants in redeeming either the living or the dead. But we speak not just of immortality but also of eternal life, and for that the gospel path and gospel covenants are essential. And the Savior needs a church to make them available to all of God's children—both the living and the dead."[34]

Although there may be many places to serve others outside the Church, there is no other place on earth where we can serve and stand in for our ancestors and those on the other side who died without the gospel of Jesus Christ. Perhaps worst of all, if we are not found standing in the holy place of the Church, we forfeit the temporal and spiritual blessings that accompany Church membership. We miss out on the power that comes from regularly and worthily partaking of the sacrament of the Lord's Supper and the constant companionship of the Spirit it promises. We separate ourselves from the spiritual communion called by the Book of Mormon prophet Enos "the joy of the Saints" (Enos 1:3). Perhaps most serious of all, we cut ourselves off from sacred service, blessings, and power found only in perhaps the most sacred and holy of all earthly places, "The House of the Lord."

THE TEMPLE

The temple is probably the first thing we think of when we read in the scriptures the admonitions to stand in holy places.

In the Bible—both the Old and New Testaments—the term *holy place* would have referred to the temporary tabernacle or subsequently Solomon's or Herod's temple in Jerusalem. But the Saints in the meridian of time would not have found permanent safety at the temple in Jerusalem because it was ultimately destroyed (see Matthew 24:15). In the Doctrine and Covenants the term would have likewise been interpreted to mean temples. Yet how can we all fit in the temple? And how could we all get to a temple when the destructions and difficulties of the last days fully come? So obviously there is an implied symbolic meaning here besides the literal physical one.

The incomparable blessing of the temple in our lives is that we don't have to physically be in it to be protected by it! In fact, we take the "holy place" with us out into the world not only in the covenants we make and the sealing blessings we receive, but also in the form of our temple garments. We are promised spiritual safety and protection when we wear the garment reverently and worthily, not as an inconvenience or annoyance. In this way we always have the temple with us. Just think of it! Wherever we are in these last days, we are standing in holy places if we are worthy of our temple recommends. Attending the temple is infinitely more vital to our last-days welfare than "prepping" for the apocalypse. A temple recommend, faith, and obedience are far greater protections than bomb shelters and guns. The latter may give the illusion of security and preparedness, but the temple and all that it does for us and to us, like spiritual oil in our lamps, will protect us when temporal preparations inevitably fail us.

> *We, when we attend the temple, can be entitled to the blessings of Almighty God. As we love the temple, touch the temple, and attend the temple, our lives will reflect our faith. As we come to these holy houses of God, as we remember the covenants we make within, we shall be able to bear every trial and overcome each temptation. The temple provides purpose for our lives.*
>
> —Thomas S. Monson, *Be Your Best Self* (1979), 56

"We need to study and understand temple ordinances and covenants," Sister Bonnie Oscarson taught. "The temple holds a place at the very center of our most sacred beliefs, and the Lord asks that we attend, ponder, study, and find personal meaning and application individually. We will come to understand that through the ordinances of the temple, the power of godliness is manifest in our lives and that because of temple ordinances, we can be armed with God's power, and His name will be upon us, His glory round about us, and His angels have charge over us. I wonder if we are fully drawing upon the power of those promises."[35]

Once we make our own covenants in the temple, we can return repeatedly to contemplate their meaning and power as we stand in that holy place and provide a Christlike service to those who have died without these ordinances. This is one way in which we help save them and they help save us (see D&C 128:18), and in the process we add spiritual oil of preparation to our souls.

Inextricably linked to temple work is family history.

Together they constitute what the Prophet Joseph Smith called "the greatest responsibility in this world that God has laid upon us."[36] I like to think that by "greatest responsibility" the Prophet Joseph meant not only the sheer magnitude of what we are expected to accomplish, but also that this work has not been entrusted to any other dispensation. It must be done by the Latter-day Saints. However, another reason it is the "greatest responsibility" is because it is part of saving our families, fulfilling the very purpose for which the earth was created, and preparing the world for the Savior's Second Coming and millennial reign. But with responsibilities come great blessings—increased spirituality and protection from evil influences of the world. "Do you want a sure way to eliminate the influence of the adversary in your life?" Elder Richard G. Scott asked. "Immerse yourself in searching for your ancestors."[37] Speaking to the youth of the Church, Elder David A. Bednar made a promise regarding the blessings of temple and family history work that certainly would apply to all of us, regardless of our ages: "I promise you will be protected against the intensifying influence of the adversary. As you participate in and love this holy work, you will be safeguarded . . . throughout your lives."[38]

With such promises, we should "be not moved" from faithfully and urgently seeking to complete this work, "lest the earth be wasted at his coming"—wasted because its purpose and our potential went unfulfilled. Hopefully, when He comes again He will find us literally standing in holy places as "saviors on Mount Zion" by engaging in the vital temple and family history work of salvation.

ZION

There is one more "holy place" that must play an essential role in those days leading up to the Second Coming and during the Savior's millennial reign on earth. The establishment of Zion has been the goal of believers in every dispensation. The Prophet Joseph Smith taught: "The building up of Zion is a cause that has interested the people of God in every age; it is a theme upon which prophets, priests and kings have dwelt with peculiar delight; they have looked forward with joyful anticipation to the day in which we live; and fired with heavenly and joyful anticipations they have sung and written and prophesied of this our day; but they died without the sight; we are the favored people that God has made choice of to bring about the Latter-day glory."[39]

In this, the dispensation of the fulness of times, revelations and prophetic discourses that speak of preparing the Saints and the world for the Second Coming almost always include references to the establishment of Zion. The term *Zion,* as found in the scriptures, has several different meanings. It is places and people. Zion was the city of Enoch, which was taken from the earth into the bosom of God (see Moses 7:18, 69). Enoch's Zion and the later Nephite Zion society in which "the people were all converted unto the Lord, . . . and there were no contentions and disputations among them, and every man did deal justly one with another. . . . There were not rich and poor, bond and free, but they were all made free, and partakers of the heavenly gift" (4 Nephi 1:2–3) are the prototype or pattern for the Zion of the last days. Zion is the holy city that shall greet the returning Messiah, the New Jerusalem (see D&C 45:66–69). The "center place" of Zion is Jackson County, Missouri, but Zion is also, according to the Prophet Joseph, "the whole of America . . . from north to south."[40] Yet stakes of Zion are found throughout the world (see D&C 101:17–21). Thus, Zion is the Church and its members. As members of the Church—members of stakes of Zion—we "stand in holy places."

> *If we are to build that Zion of which the prophets have spoken and of which the Lord has given mighty promise, we must set aside our consuming selfishness. We must rise above our love for comfort and ease, and in the very process of effort and struggle, even in our extremity, we shall become better acquainted with our God.*
>
> —Gordon B. Hinckley, "Our Mission of Saving," *Ensign*, November 1991, 59

Ultimately, however, Zion as a place, as a holy city, and as a collective people of God can be realized only "by the principles of the law of the celestial kingdom" (D&C 105:5). Thus, Zion is a condition of the heart and soul. It is a state of being. Zion is to be individual, not just geographical or collective. "Verily, thus saith the Lord, let Zion rejoice, for this is Zion—THE PURE IN HEART" (D&C 97:21). President Brigham Young counseled the Saints to have the "spirit of Zion" with them continually. "As to the spirit of Zion," he said, "it is in the hearts of the Saints, of those who love and serve the Lord with all their might, mind, and strength."[41] On another occasion, he stated, "Who are Zion? The pure in heart are Zion; they have Zion within them. Purify yourselves, sanctify the Lord God in your hearts, and have the Zion of God within you. . . . May [Zion] dwell spiritually in every heart; and may we so live as to always enjoy the Spirit of Zion!"[42]

The early Latter-day Saints weren't able to establish Zion as the city of the New Jerusalem. They weren't able to build the temple in Jackson County. They did not fully become like Enoch's Zion. Yet, they were Zion and stood in that "holy place" as they kept their covenants and served the Lord. "Zion shall not be moved out of her place, notwithstanding her children are scattered" (D&C 101:17). Regardless of where we dwell, we are Zion, we establish Zion, and we spiritually prepare for the Lord's glorious Second Coming as we are "pure in heart" and live by those principles that govern Zion. It is a "holy place" where we must stand firmly, steadfastly, and unwaveringly, "and be not moved."

Chapter 7

"WHEN HE SHALL APPEAR
WE SHALL BE LIKE HIM"

Both the New Testament Apostle John the Beloved and the Book of Mormon prophet Mormon testified that when the Savior returns to earth in resplendent glory, the "true followers" of Christ who will greet Him will "be like Him" (Moroni 7:48; see also 1 John 3:2). Interestingly, both taught that principle in the context of epistles regarding *charity*, defined as the "pure love of Christ," which among all Christlike attributes "is the greatest of all . . . and whoso is found possessed of it at the last day, it shall be well with him" (Moroni 7:46–47; see also 1 Corinthians 13). So what does the "pure love of Christ" have to do with our spiritual preparation for the Second Coming? In a word, everything. He is the Bridegroom whom we, with love and long-suffering, seek to greet. It is for His return that we prepare, as President Kimball taught, "drop by drop in righteous living." It is only through pure love— *both His love for us and our love for Him*—that we can *become* what we need to be to abide the "great and dreadful day of the

Lord." It is within the "holy places" in which we *stand* where we learn of His love, experience the transforming power of His love, and demonstrate our love. *Becoming His disciples, standing with Him in holy places, and loving others like He loves us* enable us to have our "lamps trimmed" and filled with oil so that "when he shall appear we shall be like him."

Rarely, if ever, has *charity* been cited when I have asked my students, "How do we best prepare for the Second Coming?" There is, however, always a long list of "dos and don'ts." Yet, the dos and don'ts by themselves do not disciples make. As discussed previously, devoted discipleship is more about what we have become internally than just what we have done externally. Likewise, the pure love of Christ is much more than being involved in service projects, donating used clothes and furniture to Deseret Industries, or giving spare change to a beggar on the street (although each of these may be good things to do). Charity is an attribute we possess and the pure love of Christ that possesses us. It is what we are, not just what we do. Having said that, however, there are still some "key indicators" of charity in our lives that will assess how far along the path we are in being prepared to meet the Master. The scriptures list several, but let me highlight just a few.

FORGIVENESS

Because of the increasing depth and breadth of iniquity in the world, there will be an ever-increasing need to forgive as the love of many waxes cold (see Matthew 24:12). From thoughtless offenses that increasingly lead to angry outbursts and even violence to deliberate acts of unspeakable carnage that inspire revenge and revolt, there will be need for the healing that can come only through forgiveness. Rarely are we more like Christ than when we forgive. Forgiveness gives us great power over our enemies. A stunning example was the slaughter of nine African-American members of a Bible-study group at the Mother Emmanuel AME Church in Charleston, South Carolina, on June 15, 2015. They had invited a young white stranger into their beloved church to share the study of scripture with them. After a few moments of pretending to be interested, he suddenly stood and shot them down with his gun. Unlike so many who profess religion but set it aside when it pinches them a bit, the families of those killed and the members of that church made an astounding choice to forgive an act that could have unleashed great fury, chaos, suffering, and even more death—and this at a time when racial tensions were already inflamed in America. "Love your enemies," they would have read in their studies, "bless them that curse you, do good to them that hate you, and pray for them which despitefully use you, and persecute you" (Matthew 5:44). Having studied the account of Christ on the cross, they would have known how He forgave those who nailed Him to it. They had faith in the Word on which they had feasted. They acted on it, and it made a profound difference in the world.

A year later, families of the Charleston shooting victims were still wrestling with their feelings, but forgiveness was still their choice. A *Washington Post* article reported that one woman whose mother was gunned down by the shooter had told him publicly at his bond hearing, "I forgive you." Her words had reverberated around the world. Though she still grieved deeply a year later, she reported "that she learned in the bond hearing that forgiveness isn't weak. It's not resignation or a duty done begrudgingly. And it is not easy." Yet she knew it was what her mother would have wanted. "I know she would have said, 'That's my baby. I taught her well.' Forgiveness is power," she told the *Washington Post* reporter. "It means you can fight everything and anything head on." A man whose wife was killed hadn't planned on attending that same hearing, but something prompted him to go. While there, he felt that God was telling him to forgive the young man. After the hearing, he realized that it was not for the shooter's benefit that he needed to forgive but to bring peace to himself and his children.

> *Haven't we all, at one time or another, meekly approached the mercy seat and pleaded for grace? Haven't we wished with all the energy of our souls for mercy—to be forgiven for the mistakes we have made and the sins we have committed?*
>
> *Because we all depend on the mercy of God, how can we deny to others any measure of the grace we so desperately desire for ourselves? My beloved brothers and sisters, should we not forgive as we wish to be forgiven?*
>
> —Dieter F. Uchtdorf, "The Merciful Obtain Mercy," *Ensign*, May 2012, 75

Some are still wrestling with the decision to forgive, but they know it is right because of the examples set by those who were killed. A woman whose sister died in the shooting did not feel ready to forgive, but she is trying to follow her dead sister's faithful example. "God is taking me to a higher level," she said. "If the man who killed my sister was looking for hate—he came to the wrong place." And finally, a woman struggling to forgive the man who took her little brother still advised that "people who were moved by the deaths of . . . [the] victims should respond with love. Spread the love of Jesus. That's the simplest thing anyone can do."[43]

Is the oil of forgiveness in our lamps of spiritual preparation running low, like that of the foolish virgins? Or do we have enough and to spare, like the wise? Each one of us could ask: Is there someone I need to forgive? Is there some grudge I must let go? Is there a trespass against me, whether big or small, that I should forget?

KINDNESS

"Charity suffereth long, *and is kind,*" the Apostle Paul declared (1 Corinthians 13:4; emphasis added). How we treat others—not just those we have to be nice to, like bosses and General Authorities—is an indication of the degree to which we are becoming more like the Savior. Do I treat others, especially those within my own family and who are closest to me, with respect and consideration, with the kindness that I imagine the Savior would exhibit? Do I really embody the Golden Rule in my associations with others? Unfortunately, the world today seems to put a higher premium on characteristics such as toughness, assertiveness, even rudeness than it does on gentleness and kindness. But that is not the Lord's way. "Be ye kind one to another," the Apostle Paul admonished the Saints (Ephesians 4:32). President Ezra Taft Benson taught: "One who is kind is sympathetic and gentle with others. He [or she] is considerate of others' feelings and courteous in his [or her] behavior. He [or she] has a helpful nature. Kindness pardons others' weaknesses and faults. Kindness is extended to all—to the aged and the young, to animals, to those low of station as well as the high."[44] With this in mind, as we prepare for the Second Coming, surely we should be more concerned with kindness and courtesy than with canned goods and 72-hour kits.

COMPASSION

An important dimension of charity is compassion. Although often directly linked with service, compassion is more than that. Some may render service not because of deep feelings of love and concern for their fellow men but out of duty or because a sign-up list was passed around. Christlike compassion, as President Thomas S. Monson explained, "gives attention to those who are unnoticed, hope to those who are discouraged, aid to those who are afflicted. . . . It is accepting weaknesses and shortcomings. It is accepting people as they truly are. It is looking beyond physical appearances to attributes that will not dim through time. It is resisting the impulse to categorize others."[45]

As stake president, I have the privilege of setting apart elders, sisters, and couples who have received calls to serve as full-time missionaries for the Church. One of the blessings that I almost always pronounce upon their heads is the gift to see others as our Father in Heaven and the Lord Jesus Christ see them. When missionaries are able to look beyond people's outward appearances and circumstances, perceiving both hurts and hopes hidden in their hearts, miracles can occur. This happens not because the missionaries are more skilled in teaching techniques, ask more probing questions, or possess more dynamic personalities. Rather, it is because they are more like the Savior—they exhibit charity, the pure love of Christ. Having godly compassion, they have the Spirit with them in greater abundance, and others feel it. Seeing with eyes of compassion, hearing with ears of compassion, feeling with hearts of compassion can enable missionaries and all of us to perform miracles that cannot come in any other way.

"Pray unto the Father with all the energy of heart," Mormon admonished, "that ye may be filled with this love, which he hath bestowed upon all who are true followers of his Son, Jesus Christ" (Moroni 7:48). Charity and compassion are gifts of the Spirit, cultivated by service. They are attributes of Christ that He bestows upon us as we seek to demonstrate our love for Him through unselfishly serving others, as King Benjamin taught (see Mosiah 2:17). As discussed in a previous chapter, this is the very meaning of the Savior's parable of preparation involving the sheep and the goats. When we have compassion and serve "the least of these"—when we feed the hungry, clothe the naked, minister to the sick and the lonely— we demonstrate our love for the Savior Himself (see Matthew 25:32–46). As we strive to look upon the circumstances and suffering of others as He sees them, we are preparing ourselves to be with Him when He comes again and throughout eternity.

President Dieter F. Uchtdorf testified that we will not become Zion and be prepared for the Second Coming "if we only go through the motions of religiosity. We could cover the earth with members of the Church, put a meetinghouse on every corner, dot the land with temples, fill the earth with copies of the Book of Mormon, send missionaries to every country, and say millions of prayers. But if we neglect to grasp the core of the gospel message and fail to help those who suffer or turn away those who mourn, and if we do not remember to be charitable, we 'are as [waste], which the refiners do cast out' (Alma 34:29). . . .

"To put it simply, having charity and caring for one another is not simply a good idea. It is not simply one more item in a seemingly infinite list of things we ought to consider doing. It is at the core of the gospel—an indispensable, essential, foundational element. Without this transformational work of caring for our fellowmen, the Church is but a façade of the organization God intends for His people. Without charity and compassion we are a mere shadow of who we are meant to be—both as individuals and as a Church. Without charity and compassion, we are neglecting our heritage and endangering our promise as children of God. No matter the outward appearance of our righteousness, if we look the other way when others are suffering, we cannot be justified."[46]

When we feel anxious about the signs of the times or about our own problems, we can give of ourselves to find ourselves (see Matthew 10:39). As individuals with the Spirit in our lives we have an endless supply of love to share with others in public, in private, and especially in our hearts, where only the Lord sees. In the trying days that will precede the Second Coming, as we *lose* ourselves by forgiving others, being more kind and compassionate to those around us, and serving those in need, we will discover that we *lose* our fear of the dreadful day of the Lord and *find* greater anticipation for that great and joyous day.

Part 4
THE PROMISE

Chapter 8

"GREAT SHALL BE THE GLORY OF HIS PRESENCE"

Standing on the Mount of Olives—perhaps at or near the same location where Jesus taught His disciples regarding the signs of the last days and of His Second Coming—the resurrected Christ promised the remaining eleven Apostles, "But ye shall receive power, after that the Holy Ghost is come upon you: and ye shall be witnesses unto me both in Jerusalem, and in all Judea, and in Samaria, and unto the uttermost part of the earth" (Acts 1:8). It appears that even at this time, the Apostles still didn't fully understand the Master's prophecies concerning His glorious return to earth. Having spent time with the resurrected Lord, and having been taught and prepared by Him, they may have assumed that the Lord's Resurrection was the Second Coming and that He would now rule and reign in a new kingdom. Perhaps in their minds the Millennium had begun. Yes, they had heard Jesus speak of wars, rumors of wars, destructions, and plagues. But perhaps the memory of those teachings took a backseat, so to speak, as the Savior—the

resurrected Lord, into whose wounds they had placed their hands—stood before them. It must have been glorious but somewhat confusing at the same time. "Lord, wilt thou at this time restore again the kingdom to Israel?" they asked of Him. "And he said unto them, It is not for you to know the times or the seasons, which the Father hath put in his own power" (Acts 1:6–7). Again, He reminded them that, although they wouldn't know *when* the Savior would return in glory, they must be about their work in preparing for that day.

"And when he had spoken these things, while they beheld, he was taken up; and a cloud received him out of their sight.

"And while they looked stedfastly toward heaven as he went up, behold, two men stood by them in white apparel;

"Which also said, Ye men of Galilee, why stand ye gazing up into heaven? this same Jesus, which is taken up from you into heaven, shall so come in like manner as ye have seen him go into heaven" (Acts 1:9–11).

With the announcement from angelic messengers, there was no doubt left in the minds of the Apostles. They *knew* that the Savior would indeed return again in a glorious manner. He had promised it. It was not *if*, but only *when*.

With the increased secularization of society, there has been a decline in belief in God, acceptance of scriptures as truly the word of God, and affiliation with organized religion. One of the by-products of that secularization is the rejection of the Second Coming of Christ as a literal event. Some reject the notion outright, just as they reject the divinity of Jesus—if He even existed. There are others, however, who believe in Christ and the holy scriptures yet are increasingly rejecting the literal nature of many fundamental Christian teachings, including the Second Coming of Christ. To them, the Second Coming and the Millennium are to be viewed metaphorically, not literally. In a nutshell, such people would advocate that the teachings concerning the glorious return of Jesus to usher in a millennial "golden age" serve as a contrast between a world filled with wars and violence to one of enduring peace and prosperity. Those teachings are meant to encourage us to live moral, ethical lives in order to make the world a better place for all mankind. Under this philosophy, man, not God, must usher in that age of peace and harmony. It sounds good, even altruistic, but there is nothing in the written word of God that would give support to the notion that prophets and apostles in ancient or modern times viewed these things as merely metaphorical.

Unfortunately, even among Latter-day Saints we find a growing, albeit small, number who likewise reject the Second Coming as a real event yet to occur with an accompanying thousand-year reign of Christ on earth. But a metaphorical interpretation would seem to reject scriptural and prophetic teachings, including the tenth article of faith, which uses the term *literal* in referring to the gathering of Israel, the restoration of the Ten Tribes, the establishment of Zion on the American continent, and the personal return and reign of Christ as King of kings and Lord of lords. That there are members of the Church who would buy into the "Second Coming as metaphorical" philosophy is certainly troubling, but not particularly shocking. Members of the Church, if not ever faithful and vigilant, can also be deceived (see JS—M 1:22). Perhaps this comes when patience in the Lord's purposes and timing is worn thin and people say in their hearts, "My lord delayeth his coming" (Matthew 24:48).

Prior to both Jesus's birth in Bethlehem and His subsequent appearance to the Nephites and Lamanites after His Resurrection, numerous signs were prophesied, accompanied by prophetic warnings. Just as had been prophesied, there was a new star; a day, a night, and a day with no darkness; increasing wickedness, earthquakes, and all manner of destruction. Yet many who should have known better began to disbelieve the scriptural prophecies and dismiss the prophetic teachings of their day. Those who thought that the prophecies were "vain imaginations" and that the promised coming of the Lord would never really happen didn't alter reality. The prophecies and signs could indeed be relied upon, and the promised event did occur. His coming then was *dreadful* for those who doubted and *glorious* for those who didn't. Can you see the parallels to our day?

Many have questions and concerns regarding the Second Coming. I know I do. But they do not come from doubt. I don't know *when* He will come. I don't know how all the signs fit together. I don't know how much the world, the Church, and I individually will yet suffer before that day. But I do know that *He will come.* That is His promise. It is sure, and He is true to His word.

Some time ago I had a very distraught student in my office disturbed by something that was stated (or not stated) in her patriarchal blessing. "My blessing doesn't say I will be alive at the Second Coming," she said. "We have been told that we are the 'Saturday's warriors' and it will be in our generation, but I won't be there." I tried my best to comfort her. I told her that my blessing doesn't say I will be alive at the Second Coming either. I don't think that consoled her much. I tried to explain what we know from the scriptures, and what we don't know, about when the Second Coming will occur. She was afraid that her blessing was saying that she would die young—before the Second Coming—or that she would not be found worthy when it did occur. Her mind raced with all the possibilities, none of which were good, in her estimation.

"You can't make that assumption," I said. "You can't draw conclusions by what the patriarch *didn't* say." But my words did not seem to convince her. I told her that there are lots of things about the last days and the Savior's glorious return that I *don't* know. (She was convinced of that point!)

Finally, all I could do was to bear my testimony of what I *do* know. "I don't know when it will be," I stated. "I don't know if you or I will be alive or dead when it occurs. What I do know is that it will indeed happen. And when it does, it does not matter much if we are dead or alive. As long as we are worthy, we will not only see the Second Coming, we will participate in it. We will be caught up to meet the Savior and will come to earth *with* Him. It doesn't matter when He comes. All that matters is that you and I are striving to be like Him when He does. That is what should be foremost in our hearts." I don't know if my words eased her concerns, but I know they are true! There is little profit in wondering too much about *when* He will come again. But there is great profit in continually examining ourselves: our spiritual preparation, our personal worthiness, our devotion to God, our love for our fellow men, and our hope for that glorious day.

I wonder, when he comes again,
Will I be ready there
To look upon his loving face
And join with him in prayer?
Each day I'll try to do his will
And let my light so shine
That others seeing me may seek
For greater light divine.
Then, when that blessed day is here,
He'll love me and he'll say,
"You've served me well, my little child;
Come unto my arms to stay."[47]

The Bridegroom invites each of us, as His bride, to take His name, to labor and love, serve and sacrifice, and work and worship *today* so that when He comes *tomorrow* we will be ready. It is as simple as that. It's not complicated or confusing at all. I don't know when that *tomorrow* will come, but what a tomorrow it will be! We need not wring our hands and worry about what lies ahead. We can look forward with love and longing.

When I was teaching at the BYU Jerusalem Center for Near Eastern Studies, one of the classes I taught was on the book of Isaiah. While preparing for my discussion of the assigned chapters from Isaiah, I had a remarkable experience that had a powerful effect on me and my approach to the last days and view of the Second Coming. As I carefully studied Isaiah 24, which recounts many prophecies regarding conditions of the world in the last days, I began to feel gloomy, almost despondent:

- "The land shall be utterly emptied, and utterly spoiled" (v. 3).
- "The earth mourneth and fadeth away, the world languisheth and fadeth away" (v. 4).
- "The earth also is defiled under the inhabitants thereof; because they have transgressed the laws, changed the ordinance, broken the everlasting covenant. Therefore hath the curse devoured the earth, and they that dwell therein are desolate: therefore the inhabitants of the earth are burned, and few men left" (vv. 5–6).
- "All joy is darkened, the mirth of the land is gone" (v. 11).
- "The earth is utterly broken down, the earth is clean dissolved, the earth is moved exceedingly" (v. 19).
- "The earth shall reel to and fro like a drunkard, and shall be removed like a cottage; and the transgression thereof shall be heavy upon it; and it shall fall, and not rise again" (v. 20).
- "Then the moon shall be confounded, and the sun ashamed" (v. 23).

As I cross-referenced these prophecies to others in the Bible, Book of Mormon, and Doctrine and Covenants, the gloom and feelings of impending doom only increased. Wars. Weeping. Wailing. Flies. Maggots. Flesh falling off bones. Eyeballs falling from their sockets. Darkness. Devouring fire. What was there to feel good about? Was there any reason to live? Is there any hope for the future—my future, my children's future, my grandchildren's future?

As we see many of the signs of the times fulfilled right before our eyes—"wars and rumors of wars," "the whole earth . . .

in commotion," "men's hearts shall fail them," "iniquity shall abound" (D&C 45:26–27)—it would be easy to become discouraged, even fearful. Yet the Savior has assured us, "Be of good cheer, and do not fear, for I the Lord am with you, and will stand by you" (D&C 68:6). Despite the deterioration of society, with the rapid decline of long-held moral and ethical values, the full-scale assault on religion and religious people, and the many ways in which family solidarity and happiness are being eroded, we can be optimistic—even joyous. "We are in the dispensation of the fulness of times, when the fulness of the gospel has been restored and as the world is being prepared for the glorious Second Coming of the Savior," Elder Neil L. Andersen has taught. "These are days of looking forward, of *beautiful anticipation*. These are our days."[48] I like that phrase, "beautiful anticipation." There was no fear or "gloom and doom" in Elder Andersen's looking at the signs of the times. There were hope, joy, and even excitement. How can that be? Clearly, Elder Andersen was optimistic because he knows and understands the Lord's promises. The Savior has promised us that not only will He come again, but He will strengthen and support His Saints as they face the trials and tribulations of the last days. Because of those promises, we too can and should have hope, optimism, and "beautiful anticipation." Elder Andersen declared:

"As we find our way in a world less attentive to the commandments of God, we will certainly be prayerful, but we need not be overly alarmed. The Lord will bless His Saints with the added spiritual power necessary to meet the challenges of our day.

". . . As evil increases in the world, there is a compensatory spiritual power for the righteous. As the world slides from its spiritual moorings, the Lord prepares the way for those who seek Him, offering greater assurance, greater confirmation, and greater confidence in the spiritual direction they are traveling."[49]

I sensed somewhat that "compensatory spiritual power" while studying chapter 25 of Isaiah in preparation for my class. The light of hope and optimism in that chapter soon dispelled the gloom and doom and despair that I had been feeling as I focused on the signs of disease and destruction enumerated in chapter 24. The very first verse caught me by surprise, coming right on the heels of so much darkness and discouragement. "O Lord, thou art my God; I will exalt thee, I will praise thy name; for thou hast done wonderful things; thy counsels of old are faithfulness and truth" (Isaiah 25:1). Then Isaiah identified the mighty, glorious things that God will do, as He promised, to bless His children and comfort them at the Savior's coming. "For thou hast been a strength to the poor, a strength to the needy in distress, a refuge from the storm, a shadow from the heat, when the blast of the terrible ones is as a storm against the wall" (Isaiah 25:4). As I read the following words, my heart melted. A veritable flood of love and hope enveloped me. Tears flowed freely—tears of joy and gratitude.

"He will swallow up death in victory; and the Lord God will wipe away tears from off all faces; and the rebuke of his people shall he take away from off all the earth: for the Lord hath spoken it.

"And it shall be said in that day, Lo, this is our God; *we have waited for him,* and he will save us: this is the Lord; *we have waited for him,* we will be glad and rejoice in his salvation" (Isaiah 25:8–9; emphasis added).

So many of my favorite hymns are those that speak encouraging words to the faithful as they joyfully await the Savior's return and testify of the promised blessings that will accompany Him.

Come, O thou King of Kings!
We've waited long for thee,
With healing in thy wings
To set thy people free.
Come, thou desire of nations, come;
Let Israel now be gathered home.

Come, make an end to sin
And cleanse the earth by fire,
And righteousness bring in,
That Saints may tune the lyre
With songs of joy, a happier strain,
To welcome in thy peaceful reign.[50]

* * *

Let Zion in her beauty rise;
Her light begins to shine.
Ere long her King will rend the skies,
Majestic and divine,
The gospel spreading through the land,
A people to prepare
To meet the Lord and Enoch's band,
Triumphant in the air.

Ye heralds, sound the golden trump
To earth's remotest bound.
Go spread the news from pole to pole
In all the nations round:

That Jesus in the clouds above,
With hosts of angels too,
Will soon appear, his Saints to save,
His enemies subdue.

That glorious rest will then commence
Which prophets did foretell,
When Saints will reign with Christ on earth,
And in his presence dwell
A thousand years, oh, glorious day!
Dear Lord, prepare my heart
To stand with thee on Zion's mount
And nevermore to part.[51]

* * *

Oh, how joyful it will be
When our Savior we shall see!
When in splendor he'll descend,
Then all wickedness will end.
Oh, what songs we then will sing
To our Savior, Lord, and King!
Oh, what love will then bear sway
When our fears shall flee away!

All arrayed in spotless white,
We will dwell 'mid truth and light.
We will sing the songs of praise;
We will shout in joyous lays.
Earth shall then be cleansed from sin.
Ev'ry living thing therein
Shall in love and beauty dwell;
Then with joy each heart will swell.[52]

CONCLUSION

Today as I hold in the palm of my hand my two-thousand-year-old Herodian oil lamp, I see not just an archaeological relic of a bygone age. I see the ten virgins. I can almost feel their excitement as they wait for the coming bridegroom. I feel for them and understand to some degree how hard it is to wait and wait and wait. Seeing how small the lamp is in my hand, I am reminded of the need to be ever watchful—to have plenty of oil, both in the lamp and in the vessels, and to keep refilling them because it may be a long night. My "ten virgins lamp" also reminds me of the incredible joy and celebration that the five wise virgins experienced as they greeted the bridegroom. Likewise, it reminds me of the Savior, His teachings, His promises, and His love. It stands as a symbol of hope and longing—longing for the glorious future day of Christ's return and hope that I and those whom I love will be found righteous and ready to be caught up to meet Him (see D&C 88:83–98).

"And so great shall be the glory of his presence" (D&C 133:49). "For since the beginning of the world have not men heard nor perceived by the ear, neither hath any eye seen," the scriptures attest, "how great things [God] hast prepared for him that waiteth for [the Lord]" (D&C 133:45).

Oh, what promises are in store for those who have waited for the Lord, whether in life or in death! And "they shall come forth and stand on the right hand of the Lamb, when he shall stand upon Mount Zion, and upon the holy city, the New Jerusalem; *and they shall sing the song of the Lamb, day and night forever and ever*" (D&C 133:56; emphasis added).

Oh, how I want to be there!

NOTES

1. See Spencer W. Kimball, *Faith Precedes the Miracle* (1972), 253–55.
2. Thomas S. Monson, "Be of Good Cheer," *Ensign*, May 2009, 92.
3. Kimball, *Faith Precedes the Miracle*, 256.
4. Mirla Greenwood Thayne, "When He Comes Again," *Children's Songbook* (1989), 82–83.
5. See Brigham Young, in Journal History, Volume 57 (17 August–29 August 1862), 22 August 1862, 1; Church History Library file CR 100, 137.
6. See Dan Erickson, *"As a Thief in the Night"—The Mormon Quest for Millennial Deliverance* (1998), 182–89.
7. Joseph Young, in *Journal of Discourses*, 26 vols. (1854–1886), 9:230–31; emphasis added.
8. Gordon B. Hinckley, *Teachings of Gordon B. Hinckley* (1997), 576–77.
9. This brief summary of signs preceding the Second Coming has been adapted from Larry E. Dahl, "The Second Coming of Christ," in Larry E. Dahl and Robert L. Millet, eds., *The Capstone of Our Religion: Insights into the Doctrine and Covenants* (1993), 95–112; see also "Jesus Christ, Second Coming of," in Dennis L. Largey and Larry E. Dahl, eds., *Doctrine and Covenants Reference Companion* (2012), 311–15; Kent P. Jackson, "Prophecies of the Last Days

in the Doctrine and Covenants and Pearl of Great Price," in *The Heavens Are Open* (1993), 163–81.

10. Glenn L. Pace, "A Thousand Times," *Ensign,* November 1990, 8, 10.

11. "Church Responds to Inquiries About Preparedness," official statement of the Church, September 26, 2015, http://www.mormon newsroom.org/article/church-responds-to-inquiries-about -preparedness.

12. See *Teachings of Presidents of the Church: Wilford Woodruff* (2004), 256.

13. Leila Leah Bronner, "The Jewish Messiah: A Historical Perspective," http://www.bibleandjewishstudies.net/articles/jewishmessiah.htm.

14. See Kimball, *Faith Precedes the Miracle,* 109–14.

15. Heber C. Kimball, in *Journal of Discourses,* 4:181; emphasis added.

16. Dallin H. Oaks, "The Challenge to Become," *Ensign,* November 2000, 32; emphasis in original.

17. See Ezra Taft Benson, *A Witness and a Warning* (1988), 21–22.

18. Thomas S. Monson, "The Power of the Book of Mormon," *Ensign,* May 2017, 87.

19. See Neil L. Andersen, "Faith Is Not by Chance, but by Choice," *Ensign,* November 2015, 65–68.

20. As told by a grandson, Raymond Smith Jones, in David E. Miller, *Hole-in-the-Rock* (1966), 111.

21. Ibid., 112.

22. Harold B. Lee, in Conference Report, October 1970, 153, 152.

23. As quoted in Abraham H. Cannon Diaries, January 29, 1891, Salt Lake City, Vol. 14:9; Box 5, Folder 20, Special Collections, Harold B. Lee Library, Brigham Young University.

24. *Teachings: Wilford Woodruff,* 256.

25. Kimball, *Faith Precedes the Miracle,* 254; emphasis added.

26. David A. Bednar, "Converted unto the Lord," *Ensign,* November 2012, 109; emphasis added.

27. Jeffrey R. Holland, "Israel, Israel, God Is Calling," Church Educational System Devotional, September 9, 2012; emphasis in original.

28. Russell M. Nelson, "Celestial Marriage," *Ensign,* November 2008, 92, 93.

29. "The Family: A Proclamation to the World," *Ensign,* November 2010, 129.

30. M. Russell Ballard, "Feasting at the Lord's Table," *Ensign*, May 1996, 81; emphasis added.

31. See Bruce A. Chadwick, Brent L. Top, and Richard J. McClendon, *Shield of Faith* (2010); see also Brent L. Top and Bruce A. Chadwick, *Ten Secrets Wise Parents Know* (2004); *Rearing Righteous Youth in Zion* (1998); "Helping Teens Stay Strong," *Ensign*, March 1999, 26–34.

32. Monson, "Power of the Book of Mormon," 86.

33. Bruce R. McConkie, "Our Relationship with the Lord," BYU Devotional, March 2, 1982; emphasis added.

34. D. Todd Christofferson, "Why the Church?" *Ensign*, November 2015, 108–10.

35. Bonnie L. Oscarson, "Rise Up in Strength, Sisters in Zion," *Ensign*, November 2016, 13.

36. *Teachings of Presidents of the Church: Joseph Smith* (2007), 475.

37. Richard G. Scott, "The Joy of Redeeming the Dead," *Ensign*, November 2012, 94.

38. David A. Bednar, "The Hearts of the Children Shall Turn," *Ensign*, November 2011, 27.

39. *Teachings: Joseph Smith*, 186.

40. *History of the Church of Jesus Christ of Latter-day Saints*, 7 vols. (1932–1951), 6:318–19.

41. Brigham Young, in *Journal of Discourses*, 2:253.

42. Brigham Young, in *Journal of Discourses*, 8:198, 205.

43. Bob Smietana, "A year later, families of the Charleston shooting victims still wrestle with forgiveness," *Washington Post*, June 17, 2016; https://www.washingtonpost.com/news/acts-of-faith/wp/2016/06/17/forgiving-dylann-roof-is-taking-a-heavy-toll-on-those-left-behind-but-theyre-not-giving-up/?utm_term=.479842b517b6.

44. Ezra Taft Benson, "Godly Characteristics of the Master," *Ensign*, November 1986, 47.

45. Thomas S. Monson, "Charity Never Faileth," *Ensign*, November 2010, 124.

46. Dieter F. Uchtdorf, address to the Salt Lake City Inner City Mission, December 4, 2015; http://www.mormonnewsroom.org/article/president-uchtdorf-transcript-salt-lake-inner-city-mission.

47. Thayne, "When He Comes Again," 82–83.

NOTES

48. Neil L. Andersen, "A Compensatory Spiritual Power for the Righteous," BYU Devotional, August 18, 2015 (given during Campus Education Week); emphasis added.

49. Ibid.

50. "Come, O Thou King of Kings," *Hymns of The Church of Jesus Christ of Latter-day Saints* (1985), no. 59.

51. "Let Zion in Her Beauty Rise," *Hymns*, no. 41.

52. "Come, Ye Children of the Lord," *Hymns,* no. 58.

126

INDEX